PETER COOK AND ROSIE LLEWELLYN-JONES

NEW SPIRIT IN ARCHITECTURE

RIZZOLI
NEW YORK

First published in the United States of America in 1991 by

Rizzoli International Publications, Inc.

300 Park Avenue South, New York, NY 10010

COPYRIGHT © 1991 RIZZOLI INTERNATIONAL PUBLICATIONS, INC.

Library of Congress Cataloging-in-Publication Data

Cook, Peter, 1936–

New spirit in architecture/Peter Cook and Rosie Llewellyn-Jones

p. cm.

ISBN 0-8478-1263-4. —ISBN 0-8478-1264-2 (pbk.)

1. Architecture, Modern—20th century—Themes, motives.

I. Llewellyn-Jones, Rosie. II. Title.

NA680.C65 1991   *90-8398*
                                      CIP
724'.6—dc20

*Design and composition by Group **C***
NEW HAVEN / SAN FRANCISCO

Edited by Kate Norment

Printed and bound in Singapore

For information about our audio products, write us at:
Newbridge Book Clubs, 3000 Cindel Drive, Delran, NJ 08370

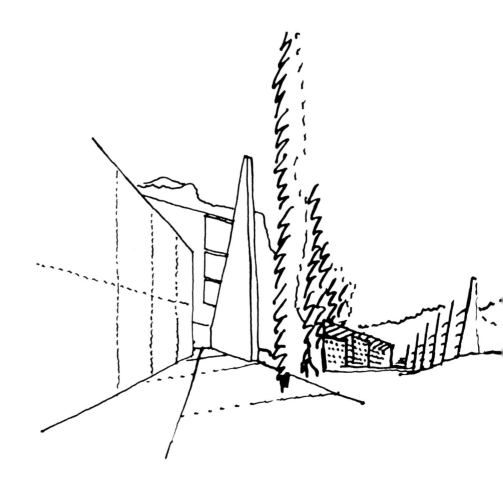

Left: Miralles and Pinós. Cemetery, Igualada, Spain. 1990. Sketch.

Title page: Coop Himmelblau. Open House, Malibu, California. 1983/89.

Contents page: Zaha Hadid. Hafenstrasse Housing Project, Hamburg, Germany. 1989. Detail of drawing.

Front cover, left: Morphosis. Kate Mantilini Restaurant, Los Angeles. 1984. Paste drawing.

Front cover, right: Christian de Portzamparc. City of Music, Parc de la Villette, Paris. 1990. View from the garden. Photograph by Nicolas Borel.

Back cover: Zaha Hadid. Tomigaya Building and Azabu-Jyuban Building, Tokyo. 1990. Preliminary painting.

Back flap (hardcover): Coop Himmelblau. Baumann Studio, Vienna. 1984. Interior. Photograph by Gerald Zugmann.

PREFACE

Forty architects from different countries have been selected for this book. They are not generally among the best known in their profession; indeed, some have not yet begun to build. Most are young, in their thirties or early forties. A few have been practicing since the 1960s but are only now starting to win the recognition we think they deserve.

The names of certain of these architects are mentioned in conversation (usually among other architects) and are known to those who prepare lecture series, lists for invited competitions, and magazine features—in short, those who are somewhere near the cutting edge of ideas. Yet these architects are typically presented together only as representatives of partisan or localized groups. This book is an attempt to integrate them into a larger context and to satisfy the need for more information about their work.

The recent demise of postmodernism, along with the increasing number of inventive, exciting architects around the world whose work goes beyond the limits of "structure," "construction," "deconstruction," or "neo-modernism," demands that some of this new architecture be examined collectively. No label could define these architects; rather, the common characteristic of those included here (and this is merely an interim list) is that they each display a certain spirit. Their architecture uses form, placement, and aesthetics in a more thrusting, forward-looking way than the work of other practitioners, which tends to be calm, contemplative, even cautious.

We want to broaden the architectural debate by introducing people who may be known to only a small group of enthusiasts. We hope that this book will serve as an inspiration to readers, encouraging them to pursue the work of these architects, not only through the written word or photographs but also through the buildings themselves.

PETER COOK AND ROSIE LLEWELLYN-JONES

LONDON, 1990

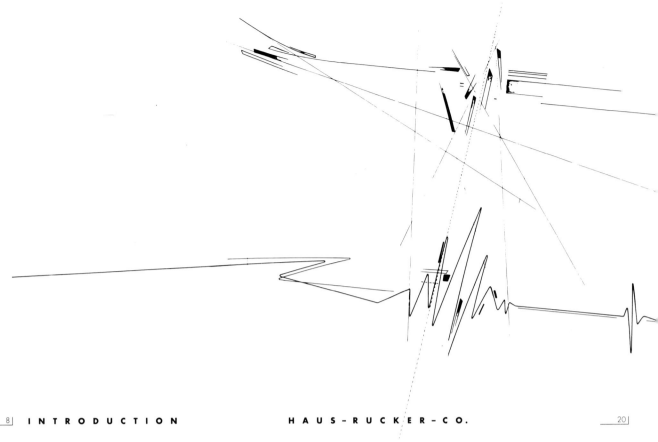

1 | Gustave Strauven. 11 Square
Ambiorix, Brussels. 1903.

_1 |

It is somehow reassuring that it is the built ideas of power and originality that survive best. Perhaps that is why in this book we end up with a very high percentage of built buildings despite the extended discussion over the last twenty years of so much unbuilt

I N T R O D U C T I O N work. Yet the trade in ideas continues, the simultaneous buying and selling of the measurable and the mythical, the drawable and the buildable, the more to feed a generation or two of architecture fanciers who endlessly voice the sentiments that architecture has lost its way, that the days of the heroes are over, and that we should all be building "sensibly." In lieu of direction, heroics, and nonsense, we must have tabulation.

Architectural criticism and discussion seem to depend more and more on the categorization of symbols. Great efforts have been made to identify positions and then to keep the protesting architects working within their assigned slots. So when Adolfo Natalini found his work exhibited in the Frankfurt Architecture Museum under the category "postmodernist," he could wearily remark that next time they should call him Chinese. Perhaps as a preemptive instinct against this categorizing tendency, conscious architecture-making in the eighteenth, nineteenth, and twentieth centuries has been full of attempts by architects to define, to underscore, and to clarify their positions, sometimes at the expense of real, integral thought. Eventually the chosen position will seem to consistently lose ground in the general debate, and the architects will be expected to switch their allegiance.

Contrary to this need for definition is the notion of a spirited architecture, a near-anarchic concept. It suggests that within and beyond the systems of architectural education and training there comes a time when the language needs to be stretched, the statement exaggerated, risks taken. There is a heady, almost irrational moment when "he who dares, wins"; when the predictable resolution of material, program, and site is deliberately replaced. In some cases it is replaced by a recognizable inversion of the typical forces ("look—no hands" engineering, "look—no walls" enclosures, various forms of illusionism), in other cases by a strange mixture of architectural devices that are the product of a creatively liberal mind.

At this moment in history we are supposed to be wary of the role of the avant-garde, perhaps because it was predominant in the early part of the century and therefore in the wrong time for us in terms of acceptable historical cycles, or perhaps because it threatens the neat structure of architectural categorizations by its maverick patterns of play. For this reason alone it merits attention in our survey of spirit in the late twentieth century. The avant-garde often set itself against the procedures of the day, as well as its icons. At its best, however, it attempted to explode the entire system of relationships: dismantling the language of criticism, the tonal scale, the frame, or the medium of transmission while affronting the eye, mind, or ear with more than a mere *alternative*. Perhaps the major weakness of much architectural avant-gardism is its habit of integrating itself back into the mainstream at too early a point. While this is understandable in that architecture is a social and useful art, it is puzzling in light of the plethora of drawn architectural statements of the last few years. Even without being partisan as to style or content, one can say that very few architectural projects attend to the question of fundamental composition or the aesthetics of the chain of events, although literature, music, and dance have been involved in just such a revolution within the same period. Daniel Libeskind, in his ability to summon up gambits that are clearly related to both mathematics and music; Michael Webb, in his simultaneous use of the commonplace actions of the man in the street (or, more correctly, the man in the device) and notions of geophysical theory; and Coop Himmelblau, in their consistent attempt to "dart" across all the carefully documented niceties of task, place, and space by capturing the instantaneous, the first gesture—each in their own way displays a fearlessness and, more significantly, a wish to bypass (or is it reinvent?) the tyranny of additive and circumstantial thinking in architecture. In this sense, they are surely in the tradition of the best of the avant-garde. We can examine their work on the level of a captured dynamic, whether or not the actual artifacts have a symbolic dynamic. Essentially, they contribute to the re-creation of the culture of architecture by concentrating upon its process.

From our historical position we are able to measure a phenomenon parallel to that of the ready transmission and distortion of ideas across traditional cultural boundaries. This condition, which can be seen as a filter that smooths the process, is the condition of coercion, or catalysis, that occurs in a *certain place at a certain time*. Because in essence it supports an elitist view of progress, it does not sit well with those who advocate modesty and servitude in architecture. It is slightly outside a purely regionalist analysis of cultural geography; but call it what you may, sudden lurches of architectural magic do occur in a particular place, and the spirit of the individuals concerned is bound up with their view of themselves *in* that place and *of* that place. In the nineteenth century we could find great cities of action—Glasgow, Buffalo, Berlin—where architecture could run along beside the audacities and aspirations of the city and therefore include a disproportionately large quantity of inventive (and opportunistic) building. Other cities, emerging as replacements of Vienna, Rome, or St. Petersburg, craved cultural recognition. Sometimes they strove to define sophistication by adopting a high style, as in the case of Brussels and Art Nouveau ʋ. In the twentieth century it has become a more furious and less monumental trade, one of money, power, and influence, with the architecturally interesting cities distributed unevenly. Any examination of these cities has to take into account the particular city's aspirations, its patronage structure and how that may be manifested, and—to use that word again—its "spirit."

The greatest cities do not fit comfortably into this scheme. New York is too supportive of the idea of measurable (and provable) success to easily handle the new at the point of pain, preferring to wait until creative clones have been bred. Paris is too much in love with the memory of its position as the cradle of the artistic avant-garde to be able to do more than host visiting virtuosi— hence the program of Grands Projets. (It remains to be seen whether these will act as a catalyst for any creative architectural life within the Paris studios themselves.) At the same time, London is experiencing one of its periodic fits of philistinism, encouraged by the Prince of Wales: any evidence of strange or inventive work is viewed as part of the tradition of English eccentricity and therefore amusing but harmless (meaning, of course, not worth bothering about).

Yet such cities possess more than their fair share of influence. Air travel and the accumulation of academies, publishing houses, and world-networked professionals feed the insidious (though creative) institution of architectural chitchat. This in itself becomes a useful structure within which to shock, amaze, and tantalize, generating a vicious competitiveness that favors the energetic and ambitious while forcing a certain conformity on potentially original work. The true investigator of ideas may hide his activities behind the mask of eccentricity, quasi-academicism, or diffidence. He may even feel an outcast.

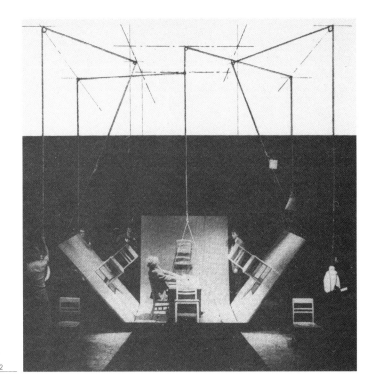

⌊2   *Elizabeth Diller and Ricardo Scofidio. Scene from "American Mysteries." 1984.*

⌊2

Two New York institutions serve to illustrate the dilemma. In the late 1960s Peter Eisenman created the Institute for Architecture and Urban Studies. Completely independent of universities and museums, it rapidly created a forum for visiting architects from all over the world to make their most sophisticated or most combative statements to an audience that was generally knowledgeable and witty. Naturally it attracted architectural academics and their followers. It also attracted students, who, though they enjoyed the style and cachet of a special institution, were conspicuously happier when the discussion was historical or theoretical than when it revolved around creative ideas that were eccentric or inconclusive. Yet spirited architecture, because it is investigatory, is very often inconclusive, shifting rapidly across territories of reference and image. Eisenman surely knew that, and he probably enjoyed the parallel discomfort of the creative visitors, who wondered whether this special New York audience really *understood*, and of the attendants, who wondered whether to take this one or that one seriously. In the end it served to preserve the notion that New York was a significant point on the map for the exchange of original ideas, but it left behind relatively few practicing experimenters for such a sophisticated city.

In 1982 a quite different institution emerged with apparently much gentler aspirations. Kyong Park and some friends created the Storefront for Art and Architecture, a gallery that concerned itself with the urban and social problems of the world, and of downtown Manhattan in particular. It embarked on a program of alternative shows of architecture and art, which have gradually moved from the work of a few talented friends of the gallery to a wider circle of those whose projects fall into the strange territory between architecture, philosophy, and art—such as Elizabeth Diller and Ricardo Scofidio ⌊2, who skillfully transcend the limitations of both enclosure and choreography and (almost inevitably) find themselves re-evoking Marcel Duchamp's *Large Glass* in three- or four-dimensional terms.

The gallery became the natural place where such diverse visionaries as Lebbeus Woods and Michael Webb could comfortably exhibit their work and where the newly emerging "architecture machines" of Neil Denari or Ken Kaplan and Ted Krueger could be seen. By now, some Europeans have joined in too, so that the refined aesthetic of someone like Peter Wilson, a strange combination of technicality and painterliness that comes out of London, is presented in a much tougher ambience. So far, Storefront has been less attractive to the seekers of fame by association. Perhaps the material has been essentially too "weird" for them; more likely it has been too *creative* in its thrust, since it generally chooses not to fall back on historical or theoretical substantiation. The work is often very self-contained, demanding an understanding by eye and by process rather than by position.

The exhibition is a curious but perhaps necessary instrument in the encouragement of innovative work. Most of the architects represented in this book do what they do despite the predictability of the work around them, not only that of the mainstream architects but that of many of their friends and contemporaries. A strange building might go up on a distant hillside or a far-off city, but not much will be known about it. A sympathetic or energetic magazine editor might move quickly, but more often than not the time is far too long between the creation of an architectural idea and its real digestion by the kinds of people whose opinions matter to the creator. The exhibition therefore acts as both a marker and a coercive event. In controlled conditions architects can make

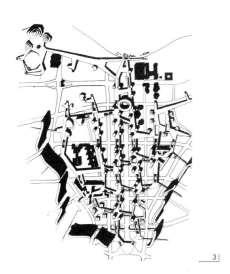

3 Alison and Peter Smithson.
Haupstadt Berlin. 1959. Central area.

a statement of position and can also serve as their own editors. They may watch the amusement, envy, or dismay on the faces of their peers. Together, a series of exhibitions can serve to irritate or encourage others to action. "My God, something's going on" can be a useful contemplative reaction.

In quite a different architectural atmosphere, the Aedes Gallery in Berlin serves these and still more functions. In the late 1970s, with the coming of the Internationale Bauausstellung (the IBA program), there was an air of expectancy in the city that a return might be made to Berlin's pivotal role in European architecture, that the ghosts of the Ring, Frühlicht, or the late Bauhaus might be honored with energy and wit. Christine Feireiss and the late Helga Retzer talked to their many friends in the architectural world and opened their Berlin gallery, somewhat unexpectedly, with an exhibition of the work of Alison and Peter Smithson—a skillful and poignant choice, for the Smithsons' Haupstadt Berlin project of 1959 3 remained one of the most genuinely original pieces of urbanism in postwar Europe. Although they were no longer fashionable, they were still highly creative; their work and the exhibition served well as an irritant and an incentive to a Berlin architectural scene that was relatively timid and provincial.

In the years since, a successful syncopation of "local" and "international" exhibitions has kept the pressure on. Equally effective —and highly puzzling to the kind of observer who wants to know only how things stand (and is therefore the true enemy of architectural development)—is the combination of established names and "weirdos" on the Aedes exhibition list. Recently Feireiss has also curated group shows in larger galleries to increase the overall discourse. So it is that several people included in this book have first confronted each other in the same space, working (more or less) toward the same ends. The exhibitions "Berlin: Denkmal oder Denkmodell?" and "Paris: Architecture and Utopia" were gladiatorial events in all but name, bringing together a cast ranging exotically in age and belief. The gallery's exhibitions of student work, concentrating on the more eccentric academies or classes, have made a similarly provocative statement against the complacency of the Berlin architectural world and its very mainstream schools of architecture. There is an almost electrical current that runs between a conversation in a school and the fragile world of eccentric or explosive architecture, and it is no surprise that several of the exhibitors in the Berlin and Paris exhibitions were to be found in student shows a few months before. On a broader front, most of the people found in this book have taught extensively, using their brighter students as perhaps the only responsive audience for their ideas.

If Aedes has taken the coercion of the local architectural force as its underlying aim, the Architectural Association of London, during the period of its chairmanship under the late Alvin Boyarsky (from 1971 to 1990), seems to have taken an almost hostile position toward a quizzical or even uncomprehending local culture. The old and famous AA school could have continued as such, leaning on its traditions and the advantages of 130 years of elitism. But Boyarsky saw it as a base for expository action. Over the years a series of exhibitions and publications has relentlessly exposed the more talented members of the teaching staff (many of them previously unknown or far too young to be known, most of them bred in the school itself) and introduced the work of curious foreigners, alive and dead. So Günther Domenig was followed by Shin Takamatsu 4 and he by Sigurd Lewerentz (the lesser-known but equally evocative contemporary of Gunnar Asplund in Stockholm). Such a series can hardly be reassuring to the designers of "Merrie

6| Le Corbusier. Pavillon des Temps
Nouveaux, Paris. 1937.

6|

5| Michael Webb. Furniture
Manufacturers' Association
Headquarters (project). 1957.

|7

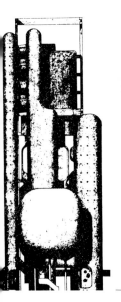

5|

England" postmodernist apartment blocks, and they studiously ignore the AA phenomenon. It is no accident, though, that Zaha Hadid, Daniel Libeskind, Bernard Tschumi, and Rem Koolhaas taught simultaneously at the AA and were given their first public platforms there, without which the brouhaha over deconstructivism and the famous New York exhibition of 1988 could never have taken place. Moreover, there is a special chemistry of nonchalant recognition that exists between the English high-tech architects (almost all of whom studied at that school) and Europeans such as Leon Krier, Rem Koolhaas, and Elia Zenghelis, who all live in London, which creates an atmosphere in which the technical and the painterly modes can be expressed with a certain detachment, a distance from the traditional centers of philosophical culture.

So it may be useful that England is removed from mainland Europe and continues to exercise a wayward attitude toward strongly held philosophical, political, and architectural beliefs. Modernism itself was late in coming and had little impact in that country, although there was much architectural free thought and natural curiosity of mind. Michael Webb was a student of James Stirling and was one of a number of people whose work at the time was termed "bowelist," referring to the gutlike sequence of bulbous spaces proposed in their projects 5|. In the late 1950s there was a re-examination of Russian work, along with a taste for the zanier side of Le Corbusier: the exhibition "Nouveau Temps" 6|, the Ronchamp chapel, and even the Philips Pavilion for the Brussels World's Fair of 1958. These were mixed with the consistent fascination that the English seem to have for Gaudi. Out of this combination came not only Archigram but also one aspect of the lyricism behind the mechanical artistry of the Peter Wilson generation. Equally important to *them*, however, have been inspirations of a less bovine nature: Duchamp's *Large Glass*, the work of Max Ernst and Kurt Schwitters. The luckiest factor of all, in relation to our search for a thread connecting real exploration and sensitivity of form, is the continued inspiration that comes from London engineers of great talent. Frank Newby, Tony Hunt |7 and Peter Rice, among others, have often taken greater risks and mastered more eccentric configurations than their architect collaborators. Rice continues to be the most pivotal figure: as the engineer of Bernard Tschumi's La Villette pavilions and many of his other competition projects; of Zaha Hadid's beautiful Berlin office building and her Hong Kong Peak and other projects; and now as a frequent collaborator with Daniel Libeskind. Perhaps the abiding contribution of London's culture toward the new architecture will be that of its engineers.

The structural dynamic has a more than usual significance in determining the essential difference between most "spirited" architecture and work that has coarsely been termed "postmodern." It is a question of space, physical ambition, and rhetoric. The postmodern condition most often depends on figuration, profile, quotation, and a compositional manner more akin to graphic design than to three-dimensional design. What links the opportunistic design of the nineteenth century, modernism, and the new explosive architecture lies outside these constraints. The new work also does not need quotation to gain our interest. In some senses it is more primeval, inherently tantalized by the challenge of capturing space and welding substance; it reminds one of the effort involved and then revels in some of the distortions and diversions possible along the way. The fascination, for instance, that Toyo Ito and Itsuko Hasegawa have with layering semitransparent skins and then drawing analogies between them and the natural phenomena

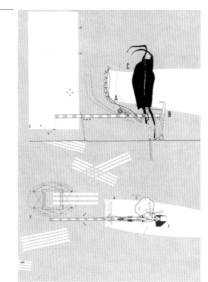

8 Peter Wilson. Competition entry
for "Comfort in the Metropolis." 1988.

7 Ian Ritchie (architect) and Tony
Hunt (engineer). Eagle Rock House,
Sussex, England. 1985.

of clouds or forests remains a primeval wish to be associated with the basic, observable elements of nature.

The distance of their city, Tokyo, from the rest of the world in which twentieth-century architecture is discussed and exchanged forces a self-consciousness that manifests itself in two ways. The first is the awareness of layers and layers of accumulated sophistication that involve craft, myth, placement, illusion, and manners. This clearly inspires Kikoo Mozuna and Team Zoo. The other is a delight in the newness and the sheer availability of the fruits of the twentieth century. Hasegawa can only have experienced joy in landing large domes and metallic hills and forests in a dreary part of Tokyo's outer suburbia, in the same way that Masaharu Takasaki must have reveled in placing his egglike form and its attendant antennae into the bourgeois area of Shinjuku in Tokyo. Of course, we can soften the argument by remembering that Tokyo is essentially a city of *bricolage*, where there are frequent shifts of reference, grain, intensity, and substance. Nonetheless, it remains the most potentially ripe ground for new and experimental architecture.

One important aspect of Tokyo's potential is the acquisitiveness of the new Japanese culture. Another, however, lies at the feet of Arata Isozaki, who, regardless of his own mobility of taste and architectural expression, has fought hard to open up the conversation. Unusually willing to introduce architects younger than himself to the world stage, he was the critical member of the jury when Zaha Hadid won the competition for the Hong Kong Peak and Itsuko Hasegawa won the competition for the Shonandai Cultural Center. His influence on the choice of judges for the Shinkenchiku House competitions has been equally important; for fourteen years this otherwise modest "ideas" competition has attracted entries from Hans Hollein, Peter Eisenman, Peter Smithson, Ron Herron, and Peter Wilson, in addition to the hundreds of students and young architects for whom it was originally conceived. It was also very clear that by confronting the tight Japanese academic scene in writing the competition program he himself established in 1975, Isozaki started a process that in the end has become two-way: the idea of designing a house for an abstract concept, a philosophical idea, a notion of lifestyle, or a definition of a point in space or time (the kind of programs that have been set in this competition) runs directly counter to the traditional notion of the clever plan or pretty elevation winning the prize. Not that graphics have been absent (we must remember the date: 1975 onwards), but the winners have tended to be those who could add visual poetry to a conceptual view of architecture.

Eventually the significant proportion of non-Japanese winners began to be challenged by young conceptual thinkers from Tokyo, Osaka, and Kyoto. The 1988 competition was typical, with a program set by Toyo Ito on the subject "Comfort in the Metropolis." That the subject was itself a repetition of the parallel competition set by me in 1978 is intriguing; it allowed for the observation, over a ten-year period of increasing cynicism or increasing wit, of the intrinsic psychology of comfort, of the reaction to city life, and of the changes in iconography, graphics, and architectural thrust. The winners were Peter Wilson from London (who had won fifth prize in the earlier version) and the young Hajime Ishida from Tokyo. The later Wilson entry ⌐8 is more spare and more elegant, more philosophical and less grainy than the earlier, as befits an architect who has in the meantime generated a whole "school" of students and has finally started to build. The Ishida entry depends largely on references to computer technology and

9   Ludwig Leo. Umlauftank, Berlin.
1972.

intangible space, with a simplicity that would never have been adhered to in the days of Archigram or of Isozaki's own excursions into robotry during the 1960s and 1970s. So Isozaki has begun to infuse a sense of movement into and out of the system. Shin Takamatsu, Toyo Ito, Kikoo Mozuna, and Itsuko Hasegawa are sufficiently unlike their European or American friends to challenge the hitherto colonized spirit of Japan. The layers of history are there as a base for contemplation, technique, and manners.

Of course, if the Shinkenchiku judges and prizewinners were listed alongside the exhibition list from the AA and then cross-referenced to Aedes, Storefront, and the Institute, it might start to look like a club—albeit an evolving club, but a network of influence and a suspicious coincidence of names. Indeed, such connections do exist; a very high proportion of these same people are teaching, convening meetings, and finding excuses to bring each other to their cities. Isozaki was in a position to bring many of them to Osaka to create follies for the 1990 Expo. The IBA program (though with a curious mixture of combatants) had the same objective, and it succeeded in showing us what a John Hejduk building or a Raimund Abraham building is like. We now have an internationalist situation wherein a series of "academies of the sky" made up of five or six people can converge on a city and leave a trail of disconcerted observers behind them when they depart. The ideals of the Weissenhof Siedlung or of the ships sailing among the Greek islands with CIAM discussions aboard have been given a curious twist. The current cross-fertilization is far more instantaneous, even if it does carry the danger of superficiality.

A very different community of architecture exists in West Germany than in Japan. For one thing, it still carries the legacy of the Bauhaus and of the patronage of modern architecture by so many cities and individuals during the 1920s and 1930s. For another, until very recently it had lost its center, and as compensation it had kept a very lively system of competitions going in every community and for almost every building type. Germany's architectural schools are large and rather technocratic, but nearly every architect of any interest has taught in one of them. Moreover, the country has so far displayed an open attitude toward the influence—even the actual presence—of foreign architects. The museum buildings of James Stirling in Stuttgart, Richard Meier in Frankfurt, and Hans Hollein in Mönchengladbach serve as catalysts if not as experimental works. None of them could have been designed by a German architect of the period, for there is a lightness of touch in the Frankfurt and Mönchengladbach museums and a naughtiness in the Stuttgart museum that are hard for the serious mind to deal with. The influence of Oswald Matthias Ungers is closer to the core of the more refined German work, particularly competition projects that receive mention but don't win (and are often the most interesting ones). He somehow extended the rationalist vocabulary into everyday bourgeois life and introduced a mix of geometrical order and heroics that has just kept clear of fascist overtones. Interestingly, he has also bred a number of ex-students and ex-assistants who now look to be creatively open and exciting architects.

Ludwig Leo, a contemporary of Ungers, sits at the opposite end of the system. Reclusive and independent and probably indifferent to questions of influence or progeny, he has created two or three buildings of outstanding power. The Umlauftank (a hydraulics laboratory) 9 and the Lifeboat Station 10 both sit alongside Berlin's waterways. The first processes the water itself and celebrates this fact by slinging a giant pink pipe on tall green legs and under a bright blue laboratory block. The mention of color is necessary

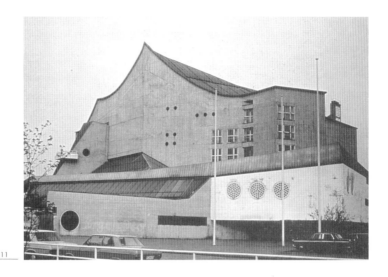

11

here, especially if we cast our minds back to the illustrations by Chernikov of objects that might be similar. The emblematic power of an audacious structure is heightened by an aggressive coding of the parts, a device that Archigram, OMA, and Zaha Hadid have also used. But unlike them, Leo is very private, simply offering the object as a working part of the system of Berlin: the detailing is basic and the building is not open to the public. On the lake, the Lifeboat Station is a wedge-shaped building with the incline descending down to the water. Here it is the products of the water—the boats—that can be hauled up out of the lake and slotted into the building at various levels. Most of the wedge is of poured-in-place concrete, and only the inclined side is complex or mechanized in its detail; it is very simply detailed, indeed almost raw, on three faces and then extremely sophisticated on the one working flank. The building is heroic but not pompous. It is dynamic but also in repose. Again, we are confronted with a fundamental attack on "normal" twentieth-century architecture.

In several ways Leo's work is a challenge. It suggests that architectural chitchat and architectural categorizations are equally irrelevant in the face of straightforward thinking. It suggests that style and iconography have only minor relevance. It suggests that the frightening (or exciting, if you like) dynamics of life can be celebrated in a direct architecture. Tellingly, there has emerged no "school" of Leo followers, and he is rarely mentioned by critics, probably because he falls into no category, does not philosophize or broadcast in any way, and creates directly out of the action of the building, a process that nondesigners have difficulty understanding.

The same instincts seem to inform the work of Christoph Langhof, whose partially underground swimming pools are of a direct quality: one comes upon the water, one comes upon the structure, one delves backwards into the ground to discover the more formal pools. The building is original without being coy: one can suddenly encounter a grass enbankment in the middle of the building without it seeming self-conscious.

One might expect West Germany, with its strong economy, its architecturally aware public, and its tradition of well-crafted elements, to be the ground upon which new architecture should flourish. Yet the innovative spirit of Bruno Taut or Hans Poelzig has rarely been recalled in recent times. Even the extraordinary liberation of space and configuration offered in Hans Scharoun's Berlin Philharmonie 11 remains a closed tradition: the work of other architects shows the Scharoun influence in shapes alone. Only very recently has the resistance to expressionism begun to break down. And it happens sideways, through such buildings as the library in Stuttgart designed by the office of Günther Behnisch. It is well known that they were strongly influenced by the work of the Vienna office of Coop Himmelblau, and elsewhere in Germany we can observe a fascination with recent Austrian work that is out of all proportion to the relative size of the architectural community of that country.

In both Vienna and Graz expressionism has been welcomed, along with a continuation of that special tradition of exquisite—even obsessive—design, perhaps too elitist for larger and more consciously proletarian countries. If Frankfurt and Stuttgart compete with their buildings, they do so at the level of patronage rather than polemics, whereas in Austria the relatively small amount of

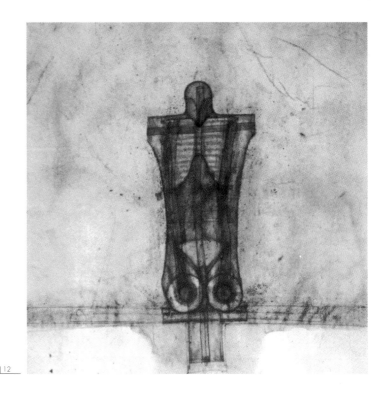

⌊12

the building program seems to have *intensified* discussion. (This is a worrisome notion for those of us who equate energy with opportunity and opportunity with action.) In Vienna there is a psychological obligation for late-twentieth-century architects to continue the sophisticated arguments of Loos, Hoffmann, or Plečnik. Add to this the ability of the quizzical, paranoiac, but sophisticated culture to look outwards in a concentrated way, as if through a telescope. So it was that the innovations of the space race and of such inventors as Buckminster Fuller (as well as architectural groups like the Metabolists in Tokyo or Archigram in London) were available for both dissection and creation. In the late 1960s and early 1970s a plethora of innovative groups sprung up: Haus-Rucker from Linz; Coop Himmelblau, Zund-up, and Missing Link from Vienna; and the pairings of Raimund Abraham and Friedrich St. Florian and of Günther Domenig and Eilfried Huth in Graz.

There was an eruption of activated arms, audiovisual devices, inflatables of all types, and megastructures. Yet not all was externally inspired, for as early as 1965 there had been an exhibition in the Viennese gallery Nachst St. Stephan (a foretaste of the fashion for art galleries to show architecture) in which the artist Walter Pichler and the architect Hans Hollein showed projects for cities. Pichler has remained a worldwide inspiration: Michael Webb, Peter Wilson, Morphosis, and Arata Isozaki all regard his work as having an enviable intensity. It concentrates on the interface of frames or armatures, often with quasi-religious overtones, and solid or earthbound chambers. In certain works, the human or animal body is interwoven with crafted metal, and bones and armatures achieve a kind of symbiosis. In his earlier work, Pichler was fascinated by the ancient cities of South America, but at the same time he was designing audiovisual helmets. As with other Austrian art, Pichler's is highly symbolic, ritualistic, even shocking. For architects, though, it has a special quality of breaking down the boundary between container and contained, as well as between the directly readable or tangible object and the referential or "haunting" object.

The power of Pichler's drawings ⌊12 is undeniable. Their oscillations between tight precision and atmospheric scribbles are as provocative as their inclusion of humanoid forms being violated by a wooden stake or a metallized limb. Another special characteristic of his drawings is the way in which they convey the idea of energy. Lines intensify (sometimes at their extremities), rasp, scratch, and scribble across the paper. Color or tone is dropped down as if blood is being spilled. These mannerisms, quite distinctive, have been formalized in the drawings of Raimund Abraham and Günther Domenig and act as some basis for the dynamic sketches of Coop Himmelblau.

But even Pichler's relationship to architecture must be referred back to the strength of Hans Hollein. In the 1965 exhibition Hollein had already demonstrated a wide-eyed cultural comprehension of both the traditions of Vienna and the artifacts of the world village. The international recognition of his Retti candle shop placed him in a position of linkage between the elite architectural circles of New York and Tokyo and that of Vienna, and it also established a level of action to which the embryo groups aspired. In many ways his role has been comparable to that of Arata Isozaki in Tokyo. His later works are too formal to legitimately come within the scope of our survey, yet as a creative and referential force, he has affected Coop Himmelblau, Gerngross and Richter, and Volker Giencke; and he has certainly been a catalyst for Günther Domenig, Michael Szyszkowitz, and Karla Kowalski.

13

Which brings us to the question of Graz vis-à-vis Vienna. There has not yet been an acknowledgment in New York of the catalytic value of Los Angeles' architectural initiative. There is general rivalry between London and Paris, but little architectural discussion. But in Austria the competitive intensity is fed by the urbanity and induced metropolitanism of Vienna and the spirit of Graz, which is akin to that of a crew on a boat (or, more appropriately to this region, a group of climbers). The Graz architecture school is implicitly anarchic, so that studios of students allow teachers to visit only by invitation, and many of them maintain a free course. The architects themselves have espoused an inventive form of expressionism that is lighter and more "constructed" than that of German or Dutch expressionism of 1910 to 1930. It is crafted and it is conscious of the natural forms and atmosphere of the land-scape. Günther Domenig, who has emerged as the key figure within the Graz School, has developed a sense of scale and control that lifts his work beyond a purely local connotation. From the point of view of Vienna, with its finesse and its depth of discussion, it would be convenient to think of the Graz work as regional or slightly quaint, but it is too dynamic and too inventive to be so easily dismissed. It is a useful conjunction, healthy, belligerent, and—in the way Austrian confrontations are—peppered with angst and anecdote.

In the ostensibly different conditions of Los Angeles, the most catalytic factor remains that of the place itself, as if the threat of descent into the sea were a kind of dare, as if the avoidance (for many years) of acknowledging a center were a mandate for anti-architecture. The exaggerated beach town has created gems: protruding from the hills are odd structures, like those of John Lautner ⌊13. A survivor of the Frank Lloyd Wright influence, Lautner is a link to the carefree, instinctive days. Yet he continues to act as an inspiration, and his work provides a clue to that of Frank Gehry and his progeny. Rudolf Schindler approached this extremity of the world with a witty adjustment of his Viennese dependence on developed crafts, improvising—or, rather, inventing—new and strange methods with lift slab concrete, wooden shingles, and bituminized cloth. Frank Gehry has inherited this quality, but also the vigor with which West Coast artists have reacted to the special mixture of light and landscape, escapism and invention.

Gehry's association with artists and their thinking is consistent from his early work through the well-known recent projects: it inspires a considered collage of unlike part with unlike part. His usual method is to make many models and to hack away at them and to glue or pin bits and pieces onto them. At a certain point there is a sufficiently satisfactory composition to justify the making of drawings. But it is not just the example of his work that is so important to Los Angeles architects; again, as with Isozaki in Tokyo and Hollein in Vienna, Gehry has given hope to younger architects, along with real and substantial support (recommending some of them to clients and passing on jobs). He is a cultural figure, raising the status of building in that city; a coercive figure, creating a virtual school or attitude toward architecture; and an ambassador for the West Coast, working by invitation and commission across the coast and deep into Europe.

As the mode of controlled *bricolage* is transferred to other talent, we can ask what is especially powerful about the Angelino model. Surely it is that essentially twentieth-century quality of equal value and equal acquisition. The plethora of forms and materials that can be incorporated into buildings in that city seems to force architects to really think hard. No longer can they fall back on

14] *Michael Belov. Ruby Bridge Over Rubico River. 1989.*

14]

the dictates or manners of the street, the cornice line, or the consistency of infill. Architects as different as Morphosis on the one hand and Aks Runo on the other succeed in establishing new and original values as well as forms for the relaxed city.

Equally inventive in its use of regional inspirations—and its ultimate progression beyond them—is the recent architecture of Spain. There a late-rationalist influence has been combined with a part-modern, part-classicist ambiguity reminiscent of Gunnar Asplund and elements gleaned from the tradition of Spanish craftsmanship to create a refined new architecture. (It is this work that is featured in the Madrid journal *El Croquis* and the Barcelona journal *Quaderns*.) Some of the best work comes from successors to the powerful example set by Coderch in the 1960s and Matorell Bohigas and Mackay in the 1970s. These recent practitioners have created a sophisticated architectural culture in Barcelona that embraces Oscar Tusquets at its more theatrical extreme and Piñón and Viaplana at its more contemplative. Their offspring, Carme Pinós and Enric Miralles, do, however, draw from far more than a regional set of influences. The atmosphere of Barcelona is by nature tough and critical. The atmosphere of Madrid is more open, but so far the city is home to no great formal talent among younger architects (certainly nothing to challenge that of Alejandro de la Sota or Javier Saenz de Oiza, both in their later years).

It remains to be seen how the global discussion of values and forms will affect that country, which is now politically and economically in a mood for expansion. In terms of the architectural mainstream, it is possible to compare the condition of Spain with that of Holland. In both countries there are a greater percentage of *good* architects than in other European countries, but is there a genuinely new spirit being expressed?

Instinctively one looks outward, both in context and in time. What will be the effects of the liberalization within Eastern Europe, for instance? We hear of talented groups of architects in Talin, Estonia, who are winning prizes in Scandinavian competitions. We see exhibitions of the so-called paper architects of Moscow, and some of them, such as Michael Belov 14], are receiving commissions. Although their work may seem narrative, romantic, and dependent on formal quotation, there is a natural wit in the Russian manner and culture that will undoubtedly surface.

It may well be that the architectural initiative of the next twenty years will come from a country or a city that has hitherto been considered on the periphery. We need only consider the important roles played by Sweden in the 1940s, Brazil in the 1950s, and Spain at this moment, and then contemplate their previous obscurity. Perhaps the hotbed of a "post-tech" architecture will be Australia (with its remarkably inventive band of architects, who seem to pick up on the technical tradition of metal buildings in the Australian outback with increasing sophistication), or perhaps Czechoslovakia or Hungary (with their sophisticated European background that has been wound up like an unused spring), or Canada. The candidate for such a role will most likely be "first world," since highly developed buildings are expensive.

In a survey like this, there is a frustration in knowing that no clear lines exist to hold or define a new experimental or creative spirit. Undoubtedly, however, ideas are being exchanged more and more quickly. The trend toward visiting lecturers at architecture

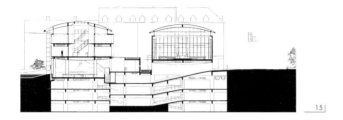

15|

schools, along with increasingly rapid means of publication, means that even places like Iceland and Cyprus are susceptible to state-of-the-art opinions and reportage. As it happens, there is a remarkably inventive office in Reykjavik by the name of Studio Granda whose partners, Marrett Hardadottir and Steve Christer, will have completed the building of the City Hall 15| (a commission won in a competition) by the age of thirty. Many observers see this building as the first major manifestation of the aesthetic and the techniques that predominated at the AA during the early 1980s. Equally unlikely in terms of context is the bourgeois suburb of Ramat Gan (near Tel Aviv) as the location for the exotic, swirling, *bricolage*-like work of Zvi Hecker, with an aesthetic reminiscent of London's NATO group. As we have seen, certain architects continue to rise above regional constraints.

Spirited architecture has to do with an approach and, equally, with the enjoyment of form, space, and materials. Anything is now possible, and a spirited outlook allows for the combination of these enthusiasms as never before.

PETER COOK

HAUS-RUCKER-CO.

Haus-Rucker-Co. is among the last survivors of the experimental
groups that were formed in the 1960s. This group of Austrians
who work in Düsseldorf have
moved far beyond the pop connotations of their early work by
making a series of structures that can be read as hybrids, falling
somewhere between architecture and public art. In their own
words, "We try to make installations that relate directly to built-
up landscape. They act as links between existing possibilities
and as a means of making correlations between intellectual
thought and real construction. They are to be seen as provisional
in the broadest sense, leading to a more distinct understanding
of built reality as well as to possible new arrangements of urban
space. In contrast to normal 'quality' architecture, they present
not permanent manifestos but provisional ones, suggesting a
skeleton for a new perception of the city."

Objects attached to existing structures and strange birdlike
sculpted pieces have progressively given way to a more austere
aesthetic—and clearer intentions. By the time of their tower
at Neuss (1985), Haus-Rucker had become expert at posing
a tantalizingly wayward structure within an apparently bland,
almost diagrammatic exterior. A year later, in a project for a
small triangular site along West Berlin's busy Kurfürstendamm,
they built the Treppenhaus, literally a house of stairs, which is
obsessed with climbing: there is a stairlike profile to the diago-
nal edge, a series of staircases folded within the structure, and
the "footprint" of the stairs and house on the ground alongside
the house itself.

In the woods at the edge of the Technical University of Darmstadt,
Haus-Rucker created a line of temporary related structures—a
"linear house"—to make a series of statements about alternative
building techniques and materials, again as a comment on

⌐2___ *Neuss Tower. Interior, view from
below.*
⌐3___ *Neuss Tower. The tower in
context.*

⌐3___

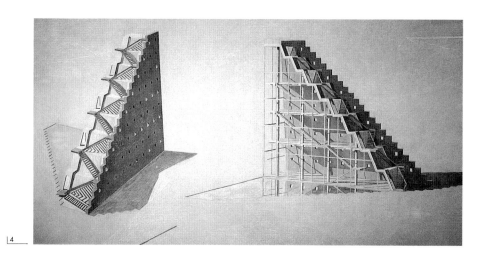

4

predictability. Recently, however, the group has been moving toward more permanent architecture, but made in such a way as to continue to provide commentary, although now different parts of the building comment on each other. So in their project for Rauchstrasse in Berlin, for instance, the issue is one of evacuation: the whole house set against one evacuated part.

Haus-Rucker thus remains at once a part of the German architectural community and a critic of that community, a stance necessitated by their work and, perhaps, by the essentially wry psychology they retain from their Austrian origins.

5

5 *Lineares Haus (Linear House),*
Darmstadt, Germany. 1986.

Laurids Ortner was born in Linz, Austria, in 1941 and attended the Vienna Technische Hochschule. From 1976 to 1987 he was a professor of design in Linz and is now a professor of architecture at the Düsseldorf Staatlichen Kunstakademie. Manfred Ortner also comes from Linz, where he was born in 1943. He studied painting and drawing at the Academy for Built Art in Vienna. He was a guest professor at the Technische Hochschule in Eindhoven in 1986-87. Günter Zamp Kelp was born in Romania in 1941 and studied at the Vienna Technische Hochschule. He has been a guest professor at Cornell University, the Hardikar School in Berlin, and the Frankfurt Stadelschule. Since 1988 he has been a professor of architecture at the Hochschule der Künste, Berlin. The office was formed in Vienna in 1967; three years later, it was relocated to Düsseldorf.

6   7   Kantdreieck Tower, Berlin. 1985. Views of model.

7

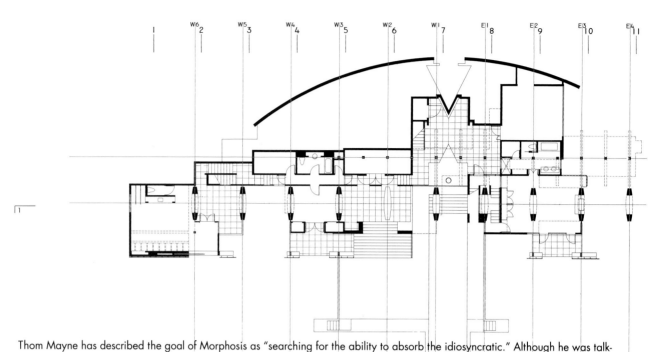

W6 2   W5 3   W4 4   W3 5   W2 6   W1 7   E1 8   E2 9   E3 10   E4 11

1

Thom Mayne has described the goal of Morphosis as "searching for the ability to absorb the idiosyncratic." Although he was talking about a particular building, the Sixth Street House, the phrase is applicable to much of the work the firm has done. Based

M O R P H O S I S in Los Angeles, Morphosis has absorbed the special idiosyncracies of the city's built culture: its impermanent beach structures, its elements built to withstand earthquakes, its "strip furniture," its fast-food architecture. But what sets the firm apart is the partners' rigorous intellectual background and their continuing involvement with SCI-ARC, which has, over the last decade, turned the tide of architectural discussion away from the quasi-historic and purely rational and toward the spatial and explosive.

The Crawford Residence, set on two acres of gently sloping land overlooking the Pacific Ocean in Montecito, California, is a beautiful example of a "beach house" that is intellectually satisfying, fully exploits the spectacular topography, and still provides a livable family home. "The building," according to the firm's description, "is about order and time and their relationship to three scales of site response: the Mercator and its implication of a global connection; a series of linear progressions perpendicular to the axis of the major view orientation; and fragments of a circular wall that form a potentially idealized notion of private ownership and other concepts associated with 'wall.' Arithmetic progressions of pylons (totems), structure, and walls determine the basic elements of the architecture."

The same fascination with boundaries, actual or implied, is evident in their Berlin Wall scheme. No longer a mere divider of space, the wall in plan becomes more like a musical stave, where the notes (or piers) along it are subtly tuned and capable of numerous

2 | Crawford Residence.
Aerial view of model and site.

2 |

1 Crawford Residence,
Montecito, California. 1988.
Lower-level plan.

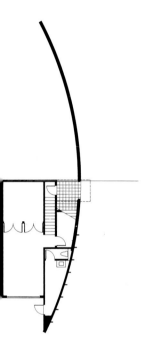

16   32

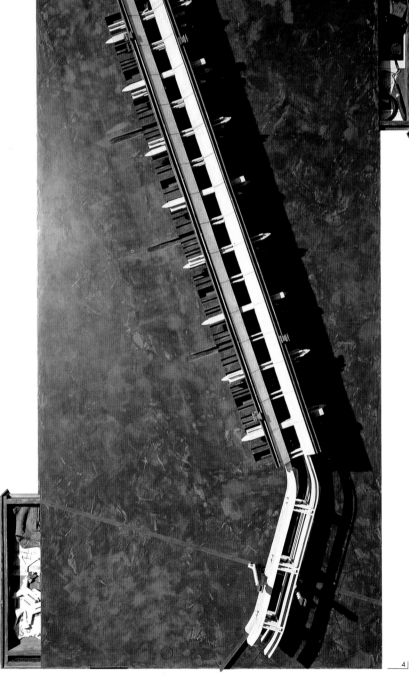

3 Berlin Wall. 1988.
Ground-level view of model.

4 Berlin Wall.
Plan view of model.

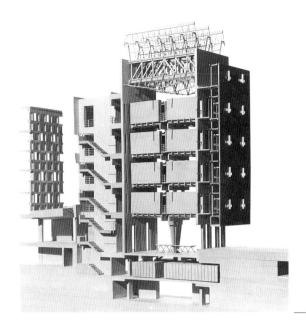

5 | Berlin Library. 1988. Section model
showing library core.

5 |

variations, sometimes triggered by the human form. In contrast, the wall's facade rolls along like
a World War II tank, even down to its "gun emplacements" and naughty swastika references. The
unrealized Berlin Library exhibits a similar spatial discipline, here tempered with a tactile quality
as the facade curves away in acknowledgement of the street pattern. The transition is marked by
a glass atrium, a successful utilization of this generally overworked feature.

In the Cedars-Sinai Comprehensive Cancer Center in Los Angeles, Morphosis faced the problem
of constructing a building that, by definition, could not be entered with equanimity. Mayne and
Rotondi produced a matter-of-fact structure, semi-excavated out of the earth, with its connotations
of darkness and the underworld. Plate glass is used to prevent secrecy and mystery where it would
be too oppressive, and the existing natural light draws the eyes automatically upward. It is a building that exudes an understated confidence in its handling of architectural elements and does not
lapse into platitudes.

There is now sonority as well as wit in the work of Morphosis. The former has come about as a
result of Mayne and Rotondi's constant examination of architecture, based on their role as both
critics and practicing architects.

6 | Berlin Library. Model.

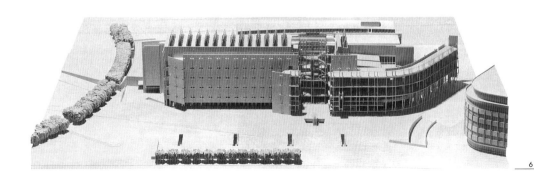

6 |

Thom Mayne was born in 1944

in Waterbury, Connecticut. He

received his B. Arch. in 1968 from

the USC School of Architecture

and his M. Arch. from Harvard's

Graduate School of Design.

He was a recipient of the Rome

Prize in 1987. He was a founding

member of SCI-ARC and has

been on its faculty since 1972.

Michael Rotondi was born in

1949 in Los Angeles. He received

his B. Arch. from SCI-ARC in

1973. He has been a member of

the graduate design faculty there

since 1975 and director of the

school since 1987. Partners Mayne

and Rotondi established Morphosis

in Santa Monica, California,

in 1975.

1

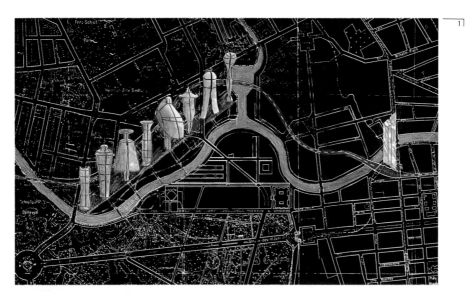

J A S P E R   H A L F M A N N   A N D   K L A U S   Z I L L I C H

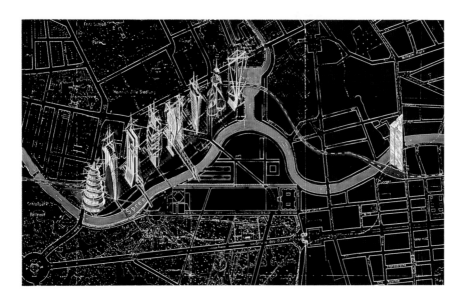

Although Jasper Halfmann and Klaus Zillich dissolved their long partnership in 1988 and are now pursuing separate

careers, the authors have chosen to review their work together. Nicknamed "Die Aufmüpfigen" (the mavericks), Halfmann and Zillich are members of a small group of German/Austrian architects outside the established European architectural community. As students the two were influenced by the English mavericks— Archigram, Cedric Price, and James Stirling. Their first projects, such as a huge model of a painted street with "curious diggings and scribblings" that was roughly categorized as conceptual earthwork or symbol architecture, were giant artworks feeling their way toward built architecture.

Halfmann and Zillich were stimulated by the fruitful dialogue of Berlin "café society" in the early 1980s and the formation of the Wilde Akademie, and in 1984 the two were commisioned by the IBA to design a bridge, café-restaurant, and orangery at Calendar Square, Bundesgartenschau, Berlin. It was a large, ambitious scheme for an untried partnership, and they responded with a sophisticated piece of architecture that looked backward to the Constructivists, with an homage to Tatlin, and forward, with slick steel-gray buildings that rose out of the earth as if elevated by some gigantic underground mechanism. The suspended girders around the central plaza, with its pillar, act as a huge, carefully calibrated sundial.

Since the two partners have separated, their work has diverged markedly, though current projects by both have their genesis in earlier, joint schemes. Halfmann is becoming more interested in conceptual and sculptural work. For the "Simultaneous Concepts" exhibition, shown at the same time in six cities, he produced a skyscraper block that was pierced, encircled, topped, and

_2| *Broken Bridge on the River Spree, Berlin. 1987. Model.*

Jasper Halfmann was born in 1941 in Germany and studied both art and architecture. He completed his postgraduate work in New York, where he had a studio at P.S.1 for three years. Since 1979 he has had an office in Berlin, where he also teaches at the Technische Hochschule. He worked in partnership with Zillich from 1973 to 1988.

Klaus Zillich was born in Halle, Germany, in 1942. He studied architecture in Hannover, Paris (in the studio of Candilis and Josic), and Berlin. He received his diploma from the Technical University in Berlin, where he studied with O. M. Ungers. He has taught at the École Supérieure des Beaux Arts in Berlin, the AA, the University of Turin, and the University of Vienna. He formed his own practice in 1988.

3 | 4   Calendar Square, Berlin. 1984–85. View of gnomon, looking north toward Café Orangerie.

shaded by a variety of different intrusions, additions, and projections. A giant hairbrush with steel bristles sits on top of the New York penthouse, producing random music as the wind blows across it. The idea of movement present in the droop of the Broken Bridge on the River Spree becomes frantic in Architectural Eros Matrix, where eight semimechanical figures whir and spin into action near the Platz der Republik, Berlin.

If Zillich's recent work looks, by comparison, more mainstream and somehow more comprehensible, it is due to the masterly, unobtrusive way in which he handles space, making it all look so easy. The LTTC Rot-Weiss Tennis Club, on a difficult, heavily wooded site, neatly tucks in sixteen courts, half of which have spectator stands around them. A center for journalists, which had to be incorporated, was slid under the raked seating of the center court, creating a gridded "light box" of interesting rooms that carries the stands on its back. The ramp that leads to the courts is acknowledged by the bowing of the "roof" and the stepping-down of the terraces. From the court itself, the stand is cool and elegant, but not intimidating.

|5   *LTTC Rot-Weiss Tennis Club, Berlin. 1988–91. Rear elevation of spectator stands showing journalists' center.*

|6   *Tennis Club. View from Center Court B.*

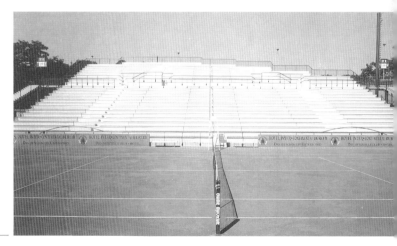

INSIDE
OUTSIDE

"Boffin: a combination of crazy scientist and shy, retiring monk. In the early James Bond movies, it was a boffin who designed **MICHAEL WEBB** a cigarette lighter with seventy-nine different uses (eighty if you include its use as a cigarette lighter)."

Is Michael Webb the archetypal boffin, or is he one of the best sensual architects working today? The answer is that he is both. As early as 1962, when Webb joined the Archigram group, Kenneth Frampton noted a "certain subversive eroticism" in his Sin Palace. Today this quality is more explicit. Webb is one of the few architects to make an occasion out of bodily functions. His caption for the design of a "his-and-hers" house, based on the automobile, reads succinctly, "Sequence: Arrive. Get up from seat. Undress. Pee or shit (toilet bowl is in middle of stair). Bathe. Sleep," and then reverses the whole process.

Yet his eroticism goes far deeper than this seemingly prurient schoolboy fascination with the human body as machine. Was it America's automobiles (not cars, an important distinction) that drew him away from England? No one else has celebrated the twentieth-century vehicle as he has. Perhaps others regarded it simply as a means of transport. Webb sees it as an opportunity, the fantasy of all long-distance drivers who pick up hitch-hikers of the opposite sex.

It is clear that occasionally he still looks back to England. His Temple Island project (1984) exploits the understatement of a small island set astride a quiet river at Henley, with a half-veiled Grecian goddess inside the temple, lovingly and exquisitely drawn. Webb is a consummate artist, too, a fact that is sometimes overlooked in the explosion of ideas, scribbles, cartoons, graffiti, and explanations that burst from his fertile brain onto paper.

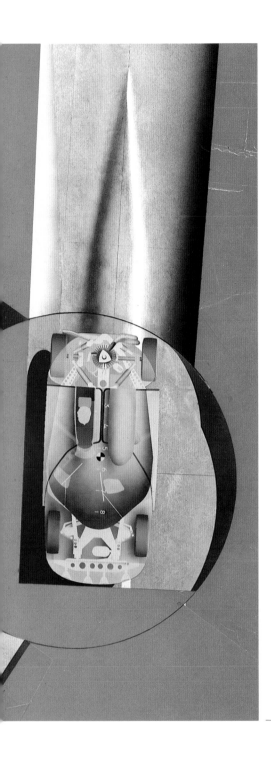

Michael Webb was born in 1937

and educated at the Polytechnic

of Central London School of

Architecture, graduating in 1962.

He worked for a number of

London-based offices in the early

1960s. In 1965 he moved to the

United States. He is currently

teaching at Columbia University's

Graduate School of Architecture,

Planning, and Preservation and

Cooper Union in New York.

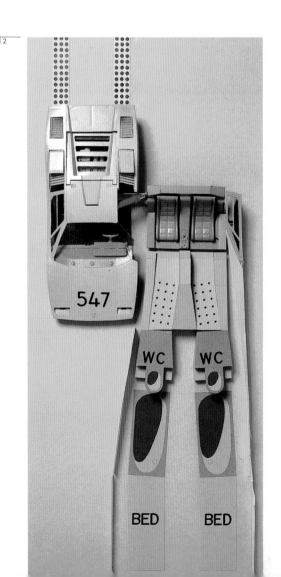

547

WC   WC

BED   BED

1| Study of a proposal for a house whereby the car, upon arriving at the house, and being subject to a few deft movements, finds itself in the middle of the living-room floor. The platform upon which the car sits rotates independently of the drum valves. Shown here in "accept arrival of car" position; drum and platform then rotate counterclockwise until inner walls of drum align with walls of living room.

2| Top and side views of a design for a his-and-hers house whose plan derives from the seating layout of their automobile.

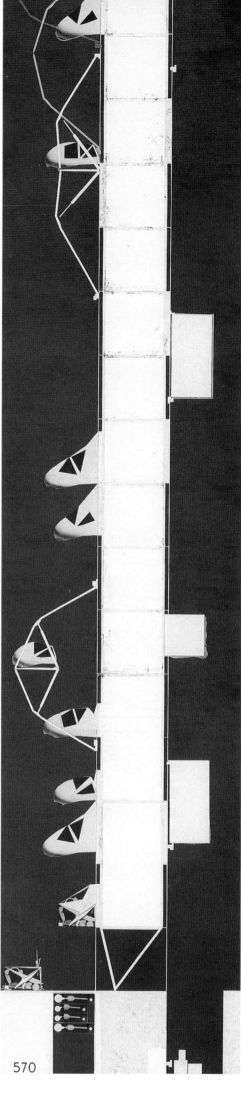

|3 The car has arrived at an apartment building. The chassis and body separate; the chassis goes to a rack storage system, and the body is hoisted up into the sky through a crawling cage structure, where it flowers out to become one with the apartment unit.

Another neglected facet—one not so obvious from the drawn work but reiterated in lectures and written essays—is his fascination with numbers, with grids and the invisible ley lines radiating to and from his objects. Neither the Henley goddess nor its submarines nor the automobiles arrived where they are by chance; they are there because of a complicated series of calculations, which, when explained, indicate that this was the only place where they could logically be. While it takes a mathematician (and sometimes, as Webb himself admits, an act of faith) to appreciate fully the reasoning behind his placement of objects, it is clear that the location is as important as the finished image.

Today he describes himself as "having been not exactly what you'd call au courant in the last two decades, during which time po-mo and decon waxed and waned. The work of the likes of Webb, back-room boy, boffin, etc., that part of it that concerned the automobile/house relationship, could be retreaded, dusted off as if were, and served anew, this time as a try-anything-type answer to mitigate the coming disaster homo-not-so-sapiens has cooked up, namely the atmospheric warming."

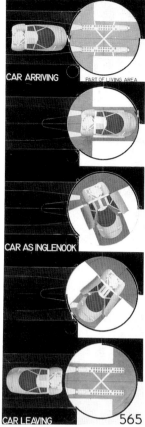

CAR ARRIVING   PART OF LIVING AREA

CAR AS INGLENOOK

CAR LEAVING   565

5   More studies for the Drive-in-Housing series. Sequence from top: 1. Car arrives in driveway, rotating insulated door in closed position, platform ready to receive car. 2. Door rotates counterclockwise, allowing car to enter. 3. Platform and door rotate clockwise (on the same spindle). Car is now part of the living-room furniture, you might say. 4. Door now rotates counterclockwise, platform clockwise. 5. Door in open position, platform aligns with roadway, allowing car to leave.

4   A garden pavilion, comprising one fixed floor slab and one fixed wall panel (shown in white). Retractable skins crawl into place as the exigencies of climate demand; they lean against each other for support, and when not in use they flop down and play dead—crazy to have each skin rigid and self-supporting.

Coop Himmelblau is outstanding not only because of the extra-ordinary power and verve of their work but also because they **C O O P   H I M M E L B L A U** are one of the few late-1960s groups who have survived and continue to produce architecture marked by an ever-increasing level of experimentation.

The early work of Coop Himmelblau, headed by Wolf Prix and Helmut Swiczinsky, was in the idiom of the other groups of the time—inflatable bubbles and urban ephemera—though their versions were always highly elegant and visually memorable. Despite the urbanity of their Reiss Bar in Vienna (a mutation of Pop imagery and memories of Adolf Loos), their contemporary statements are essentially questioning: "If there is a poetry of desolation, then it is the aesthetic of the architecture of death in white sheets. Death in tiled hospital rooms. The architecture of sudden death on the pavement. Death from a rib cage pierced by a steering column. The path of a bullet through a dealer's head on 42nd Street. The aesthetic of the architecture of the surgeon's razor-sharp scalpel. The aesthetic of peep-show sex in washable plastic boxes. Of broken tongues and dried-up eyes. And that is how buildings have to be. Unpleasant, rough, pierced. Blazing. Like an erected angel of death." (*The Poetry of Desolation,* 1978)

Later their work began to take on a more twisted, spiky, frenzied form. In 1980 they were invited by Günther Domenig to make an action at the Technical University of Graz, where he had just been appointed professor. At 8:35 p.m. on December 12, they ignited a distorted steel structure fifty feet high and weighing one and a half tons.

"You can judge just how bad the '70s were by looking at the period's super-tense architecture. Opinion polls and a complacent democracy live behind Biedermeier facades. But we don't want

1   Baumann Studio, Vienna. 1984.
Interior.

2   Baumann Studio. Interior,
showing stairs in raised position.

3   Baumann Studio. Front facade
and preliminary sketch.

3

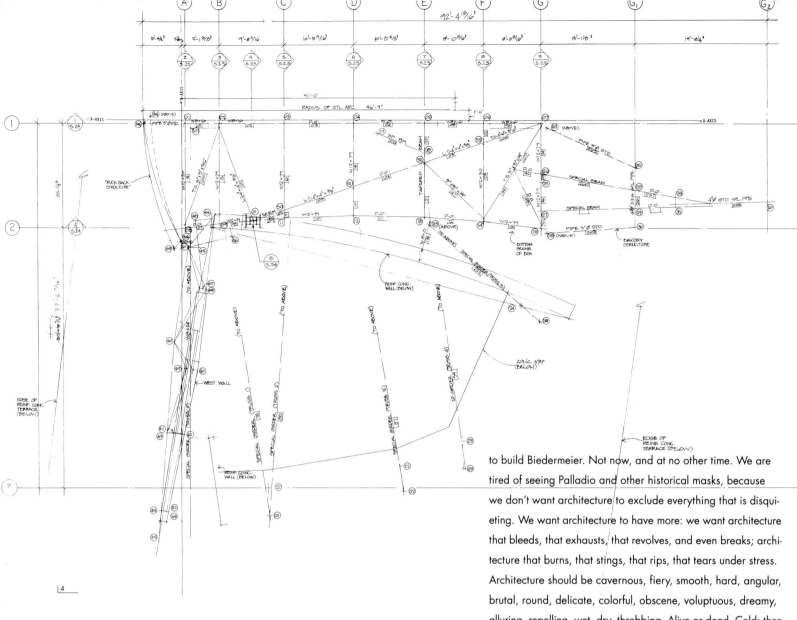

`|4`

`5`

to build Biedermeier. Not now, and at no other time. We are tired of seeing Palladio and other historical masks, because we don't want architecture to exclude everything that is disquieting. We want architecture to have more: we want architecture that bleeds, that exhausts, that revolves, and even breaks; architecture that burns, that stings, that rips, that tears under stress. Architecture should be cavernous, fiery, smooth, hard, angular, brutal, round, delicate, colorful, obscene, voluptuous, dreamy, alluring, repelling, wet, dry, throbbing. Alive or dead. Cold: then cold as a block of ice. Hot: then hot as a blazing wing." (*Architecture Must Blaze,* 1980)

The Red Angel Bar in Vienna, with its red line creeping out into the street, was a foretaste of architecture that stings. By 1984, in the Baumann Studio, the entrails had become a gyrating composition of bridges, platforms, and a lift-up staircase leading out into the street. Close inspection of their newer, larger work reveals additions to their well-known vocabulary of jabs, spikes, and flying chords, seen in the controlled "etching" of a large shed (in the Funder Factory, 1988–89) or the "layering" of folded, solid, and sheetlike surfaces over one another (in the rooftop remodeling for a lawyer in Vienna, 1989).

The restructuring of the Ronacher Theater in Vienna and the design of the Open House near Los Angeles involve the vision of a vehicular object on the verge of separating from the grand city bulk (in the case of the theater) or from the ground (in the case of the house). A key to the power and consequence of such inspired work lies in the group's ability to capture in the built work most of the actual lines of the earliest sketches, which themselves have great clarity and nerve.

Wolf Dieter Prix was born in

1942 in Vienna, and Helmut

Swiczinsky was born in

1944 in Poznán, Poland. Coop

Himmelblau was formed in

1968 and is based in Vienna.

|6|

|4| Open House, Malibu,
California. 1983/89. Coordinate
plan, showing structural system
defined by chord lines and
coordinate points.

|5| |6| |7| Open House. Model.

|7|

2 Underground Berlin.
Sector 8751, Quadrant 1 (near the
Alexanderplatz). Inverted tower and
bridge living labs.

LEBBEUS WOODS

2

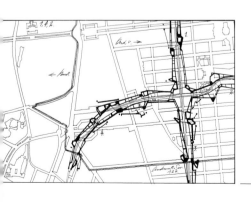

1

1 Underground Berlin. 1988.
Composite plan: surface and
underground Berlin (west and east).

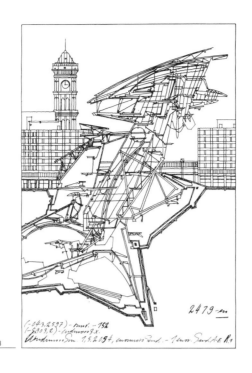

3 — Underground Berlin.
Alexanderplatz projection tower,
longitudinal section.

4 — Underground Berlin. Model of
projection tower.

To describe Lebbeus Woods as an experimental architect is
merely to skirt the edge of an astonishing range of work that
pours from his pen. He is not only
a highly skilled artist but also a poet, a philosopher, a mathematician, and a theorist. Trained in a conventional setting and
having worked as a practicing architect for a decade, he is
highly respected though still comparatively unknown. His work,
both written and drawn, demands immense concentration.
His manuscripts, which have occasionally been reproduced, are
those of some medieval geomancer striving to make sense of
observed phenomena by words and numbers.

His stance, like that of the figures who inhabit his work, is heroic.
Woods says that architecture is, quite simply, "supreme, the
highest and noblest activity of individuals and their civilization."
His is a utopian, idealistic philosophy, but one tempered with
pragmatism. He believes that architecture can instruct us how
to live but that it is still for individuals to determine how they
will go forward in this new age. "The function of a space
only exists when we act in that space," Woods says, echoing
Borges's fantasy that buildings remain only as long as we
remember them.

Underneath the divided Berlin of the 1980s, Woods envisioned
a parallel city built by people who wanted to escape from
politics. Inverted towers mimic life above ground, but, strangely,
more energy flows upward from the earth's substrata. Tectonic
movements cause the steel plates of the structures to vibrate
gently together, producing an earthly music. In places, these
underground towers have pierced the streets of the city, soaring
upward between the gray tower blocks, declaring that people
can change their environment, their political system, their lives
(this was in 1987).

Lebbeus Woods was born in 1940 in Lansing, Michigan. He was educated at Purdue University School of Engineering and the University of Illinois School of Architecture before joining the firm of Kevin Roche John Dinkeloo and Associates, where he was coordinator of design and construction for the Ford Foundation Headquarters in New York. After several years of private practice in the Midwest he returned to New York in 1976. He is currently a visiting professor of architecture at Cooper Union. In 1988 he founded (with Olive Brown) the Research Institute for Experimental Architecture, of which he is director.

| 5

| 5 | 6   *Aeroliving-laboratory, Aerial Paris Project. 1989. (Model by Christopher Otterbine)*

|7

The idea of "geomagnetic aeroliving-laboratories" arose
from Woods's Centricity project, a sustained concept of semi-
autonomous centers held together in a loose network, "a web-
bing of cycles intersecting in space and time." Woods sees
these centers as "home laboratories or laboratories that are
homes," where experiments in living can take place. Two of
the laboratories have broken loose and are floating in space,
like skulls or insects, their riveted steel plates the carapace.

Because of his striking graphic skills, Woods is often asked by
other architects to provide perspective drawings for their
schemes. His work is always recognizable, but it is only in his
own fantastic imaginings that we hear the music of the spheres.

Kikoo Mozuna is one of the most original Japanese architects of his generation, and, like many of his contemporaries, he has

KIKOO MOZUNA

been involved in the search for a truly Japanese style, of both thinking and expression. There is a fearlessness in his work that comes from a complete mastery of sculptural elements, but its power comes from his philosophical and mystical nature.

Mozuna's Kushiro City Museum is a geometrical tour de force, with exceptionally exciting interiors, especially around the main staircases, where an apparently solid and complete shell is exploded at the core. In the smaller Kushiro Marsh Museum, Mozuna again displays his abilities with geometry and light. Architecture here is brought into a strange territory: of scale-lessness, of intangibility, and of curious references (we cannot identify its building "type"; we cannot identify any of the components of doors, windows, or the like).

The strongly geometrical arches of the Higashi Junior High School are set onto a more conventional base than in the museums, but they are then revealed to the sky: in fact, the central cut of open space and the arches overhead are more reminiscent of a ruined church than of a high school. In a later design, that for the Unoki Elementary School, the geometrical action rests in the basic disposition of parts: a large circular ring is linked to a long, low block by a bridge building. It is in the outcroppings that the building becomes unorthodox. These are sometimes informal, and towers and deformations of the roof occur everywhere.

The giant Fisherman's Wharf project for Hokkaido promises to be a summary of Mozuna's ideas to date. In 1987 he designed a brilliant scheme for the Kawasaki Information City competition, in which the philosophies and traditions of old Japan were woven

2   *Marsh Museum, Kushiro, Hokkaido, Japan. 1984. Exterior.*

3 *Marsh Museum. Interior view, looking toward roof.*

3

4   *Higashi Junior High School, Hokkaido, Japan. 1985. Detail of arches.*

5 *Higashi Junior High School. Aerial view.*

Kikoo Mozuna was born

in Kushiro, Hokkaido, Japan,

in 1941, and received his B. Arch.

from the University of Kobe in

1965. He set up his own practice

in 1976.

6 *Unoki Elementary School,
Akita, Japan. 1988. Overall view.*

7 *Unoki Elementary School.
Entrance.*

8 *Unoki Elementary School.
Courtyard.*

6

7

together with science-fiction-type dreams and beautiful drawing.
The fact that the project was buildable revealed Mozuna's talents as an urban-scale thinker. A close look at the Fisherman's
Wharf suggests not only the domed and geometricized forms
his other work might lead us to expect but also a scale of activity
that is cleverly modulated to easily distinguish the parts, as
well as a stunning design for the interior.

8

9 *Fisherman's Wharf, Hokkaido,
Japan. 1990. Model.*

9

KAPLAN / KRUEGER During the last five years a series of kinetic objects has emerged from the laboratory/workshop of Kaplan/Krueger, two New York–based social scientists turned architects turned sculptors. Installed in galleries and universities, the objects—which present preposterous combinations of recycled technological artifacts—challenge received opinions on urban issues and conventional ideas of space, generally disturbing, amusing, and provoking their viewers. While kinetic sculptures of the 1960s were usually regarded only as curiosities, these communicate didactic messages on how we organize society and politics, and they are to be taken more seriously.

Ted Krueger and Ken Kaplan have fifteen years of clinical and research experience behind them. They formed their professional partnership in order to design and fabricate kinetic sculpture that would express their ideas, which arose in part from earlier projects, such as a study of urban issues in the wilderness of Alaska (where Krueger traveled on a fellowship).

The two men, who are theorists, not builders, present an alternative to traditional architectural practice, setting up paradigms but providing no easy responses. In their laboratory they investigage materials, explore methods of fabrication, and build prototypes. Works are constructed partially from "found" objects—such detritus of the late-twentieth-century technological age as the intestines of old photocopiers or the limbs of laser printers. (An organization even exists to distribute this mechanical debris to *bricolage* artists.)

Their larger installations are usually cities. Oilcan City, which uses components from photocopiers and motorcycles, had its origins in a group of specialized platforms for telecommunications and transportation, aquaculture and off-shore mining. But in a parable

⌐3

Ken Kaplan was originally trained
as a psychiatric social worker
at New York University, and Ted
Krueger got his B. A. in sociology
at the University of Wisconsin.
Both Kaplan and Krueger graduated from the Columbia University
Graduate School of Architecture,
Planning, and Preservation
in 1984. After working in various
architecture offices, the two
founded Kaplan/Krueger Research
and Development in 1985.

⌐1⌐ Renegade Cities
(Oilcan City). 1989. One of
a series of installations for the
Storefront for Art and Architecture,
New York. Disassembled
components from photocopiers,
motorcycles, and materials-
handling equipment are attached
ad hoc to a frame.

⌐2⌐ Renegade Cities
(Roll-a-Text). 1989. Fifty statements,
representing a wide variety of
philosophical positions, enwrap
an aluminum cylinder whose two
parts counter-rotate.

⌐3⌐ Bureau-Dicto City.
1989. The analogue consists of
automotive and sonar aluminum
castings combined with a
welded-steel pencil-rod frame
skinned with black latex rubber.
On the underside of this "helmet"
are six head compartments
supplied with speakers, broad-
casting a loop of Tibetan Buddhist
chants.

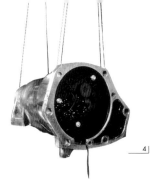

4

4 Renegade Cities
(Pig Heads). 1989. Two suspended
aluminum automotive castings
confront each other.

for our times, as the story is told in the accompanying text, the inhabitants of the city found that tourism was a more profitable sideline, multinationals moved in to exploit the idea and evade taxes, and the original pioneers began to think it was time to move on. There is a strong storyline to all of Kaplan/Krueger's urban projects. Unlike Oilcan City, Avalanche City survives by camouflage and antisocial behavior. It is located somewhere in the mountains, and the nosy visitor who gets past the electronic eye will probably set off a booby-trapped rockslide.

Renegade City (a series of dynamic sculptures), on the other hand, proposes a new type of aquatic city sited off the coast of Alaska, an affiliation of mobile communities that have come together, perhaps temporarily, in pursuit of common objectives. The project focuses on psychological, social, and ideological propositions about settlements, rather than formal concerns, but it is presented as a prototype for future cities in isolated environments. "It is a speculation about living beyond the confines of current political orthodoxy, centralized and slow-footed, unable to monitor rapid cultural and technological changes," says the text. Like Kaplan/Krueger's other works, Renegade City prescribes no utopian solutions but casts a critical eye on man-made structures and suggests how things could be. Though not exactly architecture, their work is a blueprint for the thinking urbanist.

5⌐

5⌐ *Unnamed Machine.*
1987. Commissioned by Columbia
University for the exhibition "Installed
Mechanisms."

1|

The Munich-based architects Doris and Ralph Thut have the
gift of expressing radical ideas in a quiet, workmanlike way.

D. + R. THUT If this has not led to headline-grabbing architecture, it
has resulted in innovative housing that creates intimate spaces
through the play of light and shadow.

Their first major scheme, in 1971, was an apartment block on
Genterstrasse, Munich, which was designed to accommodate
both the private needs of the traditional family and more public,
communal needs. The housing units—arranged around a core
of nursery rooms, a swimming pool and sauna, basement
garages, and a community area—consist of living and kitchen
spaces with a central prefabricated iron staircase leading up to
bedrooms, a study, and a bathroom. The structure is a prefabricated reinforced-concrete skeleton with floor and ceiling slabs,
gypsum-block partitions on steel frames, external walls with steel
window frames, and corrugated-aluminum sheeting on the side
walls. The finished scheme was dubbed the "Meccano" building because of the way different components were slotted into
each other, providing add-on flexibility. Although the concept
could have led to a rigid, standardized building, it was exploited
to give the basic framework sufficient variation and allow for
individual identification. The play of public against private
and light against shadow was achieved through the use of mesh
screens and balconies and clear or opaque glass panels.

The same concerns are evident in a similar commission for
housing for six families in Munich-Perlach. Again a steel framework is employed, but this building is less finished, with timber
cladding and corrugated-iron panels giving the impression
of the American West. Even before ecological issues were so
fashionable, the building utilized solar energy, with a glazed
conservatory running the entire length of the rear facade and

Doris Thut was born in 1945,

Ralph Thut in 1943. They both

studied at the Academy for Built

Art in Vienna and Munich,

graduating in 1968. For the next

two years they worked together

on a housing project in Munich,

where they formed the D.+ R. Thut

office in 1972. The following

year they won the International

Architecture Prize from the Bayer

AG Company in West Germany,

and the German Architecture

Prize in 1979. They exhibited in

the Paris Biennale in 1982 and

taught at MIT as guest professors

in 1985.

3 *Apartment House, Munich-Perlach. East facade.*

3

4 *Public Housing, Max Planck Strasse, Erding, Germany. 1982–84. South facade.*

4

a pitched roof serving as heat collector at the front. The timber deck, or play area, beyond the conservatory provides the link between house and garden.

With their scheme for public housing on Max Planck Strasse in Erding, the partnership is in good form again. Designing a building in a new residential district at the edge of the city meant bridging the gap between town and country. This has been achieved with a long, low terrace structure that has over-hanging balconies and wide walkways, creating a light and spacious atmosphere. The gently pitched roofs lead the eye toward the neighboring forest, and the timber detailing over the veranda recalls a rustic past.

5

5   Public Housing. North facade.

_1_

Christian de Portzamparc was one of the first of the new wave
to emerge from the shadow of Le Corbusier, who dominated

C H R I S T I A N   D E   P O R T Z A M P A R C

French architecture, even after his death, for thirty years or
more. Although Portzamparc's exteriors may veer toward the
Corbusian—in their handling of light and sculptural forms, their
rationalist grids, regular glazing, and flat roofs—behind these
severe facades, and sometimes built into them, archetypal elements are integrated with great fluidity and confidence. The
interior features are almost disassociated from what the visitor
standing outside might expect.

The School of Dance for the Paris Opera at Nanterre was a
liberating project for an architect who had previously worked
within very tight spaces on crowded Paris streets. "For the first
time, disengaged from urban constraints, I felt free," he says.
He approached the program with the philosophical considera-
tions typical of an aristocratic French intellectual with a passion
for the arts. "I wanted to find out how the feelings of the pupils
corresponded to the different rhythms of the day." The result
is a three-in-one building: a boarding school for 150 pupils,
twelve dance studios, and an auditorium and stage. Each section
is differentiated by changing roof levels, but the whole is articulated by a remarkable circular staircase that swoops up from
the double-height glazed entrance foyer. Described by one critic
as a "cage of glass . . . set in music," the staircase allows the
observer to see into all parts of the school while still feeling
sheltered. It also reveals the transition from the town of Nanterre
to the parkland behind the school, through a series of land-
scaped planes and backdrops that fade into the distance. Sensi-
tive to the needs of young dancers, Portzamparc has created
a building rich in contrast, where "stability and movement are
everywhere coexistent."

_2_

_2___ *School of Dance. Detail of*
atrium staircase.

_3___ *School of Dance. Student*
entrance.

_3_

4

4 *School of Dance. Detail of atrium
from entrance courtyard.*

Christian de Portzamparc

was born in Morocco in 1944.

He studied at the École des Beaux-

Arts, Paris, in the studio of Georges

Candilis. His first project, in 1971,

was the Green Tower, an installa-

tion in the countryside at Marne-

la-Vallée. He was elected to the

National Commission of Art and

Literature in 1987, and his School

of Dance at Nanterre, completed

in 1988, received the Silver

Set Square award from an inter-

national jury for the best building

and best workmanship in France.

5   City of Music, Parc de la Villette, Paris. 1990. View from the garden.

6   City of Music. Interior of recital hall.

Portzamparc works closely with musicians and dancers. Nureyev was involved with the dance school; Pierre Boulez was an advisor on the concert hall in the City of Music project for the Parc de la Villette, Paris. The City of Music is a two-unit building, divided by a formal planted square, the Place aux Lions. The east unit, still to be completed, houses rehearsal rooms, an amphiteater, a music museum, a contemporary music center, student accommodations, and shops. These elements wrap themselves around the central concert hall in a powerful spiral, bisected by the "street of music," a corridor terminated by a gridded gateway, an overly familiar device for a usually innovative architect. But the ultimate success of the building will be determined by its audience.

"Architecture is a public art that presupposes legitimacy," says Portzamparc. "Everything depends on how it will be interpreted. For architecture is fundamentally an art for illiterates. In transforming the countryside, it uses a communication as important as the information carried by words, language, books, the cinema, and television. . . . As I am confronted with more and more important schemes in my own work, I tend to become more personal: to move forward toward more plasticity, to renew my old penchant for the baroque."

7   *City of Music. "La Loge" under the wave.*

8   *City of Music. Main elevation, Avenue Jean Jaures.*

1┘

"What you have to remember about Christoph," says his former partner, Pascal Schöning, "is that he is Austrian. Austria is near Hungary, and they are very, very wild there; some of the wildness has affected him." This seems a strange statement at first, for

C H R I S T O P H L A N G H O F Langhof has chosen to settle in Germany and appears to be an ordered kind of person. Certainly his realized buildings there look well mannered and considerate. The structures are built into the earth in areas of natural beauty to preserve a green environment. Many of the buildings are for public use, like the swimming pools at Kreuzberg, in one of Berlin's problem districts, and the Horst Korber Sports Center near the site of the 1936 Olympic Games, also in Berlin.

But a closer examination reveals that they are truly wild, anarchic structures, with their meshes of girders, weird snaky ducts, avenues of "trees" with angular branches of copper tubing, and giant spinning-top-shaped pylons. Langhof regards each program as a challenge to show that good architecture can deceive the eye into making more of a space than its physical dimensions would seem to allow. He felt that the main covered swimming pool, for example, was "too long, too wide, and too low." The obvious solution would have been to increase the height of the hall until the proportions were correct, but this was not possible because of financial constraints. What he did was to "use architecture to cancel out the disadvantage of the wrong proportions and maybe even turn it into an advantage": he obscured the ceiling height with ventilation ducts, light fixtures, and girders, some of which hang so low they seem not to be part of the construction. "Parts of the golden structure," he says, "are sunlit by day and floodlit by night, others are in the shadows and seem dark and thick. It is difficult to estimate the height, width, and depth of the room."

2┐

2┐ *Gorlizter Swimming Pools. Interior of the main hall with the golden structure.*

Born in 1948 in Linz, Austria,

Christoph Langhof studied at the

Technische Hochschule Vienna

and with Hans Hollein at the

Academy of Fine Arts, Düsseldorf.

His postgraduate work was with

Ludwig Leo at the Academy of Fine

Arts, Berlin. In 1978 he established

his own practice in Berlin and two

years later set up the Architektur

Labor there with Pascal Schöning.

He is a founding member of the

Wilde Akademie Berlin. He has

taught at the AA in London as a

unit master for the last three years.

3 *Gorlizter Swimming Pools. Detail
of the interior.*

The Sports Center is partially sunken into a park in a luxurious residential area of West Berlin. "Many tons of concrete were poured into the foundation, the walls, and the floors. It all looks pretty harmless." But the extraordinary roof immediately attracts attention. Made of steel and suspended from eight pylons, it is curved on both sides and "hovers" over the floor of the hall. There are 420 dome-shaped skylights, which can be opened in fine weather. Each pylon has five branches, linked by cables under tension. The cables are anchored to the building and support the roof. The hundred-foot-high pylons tower over the treetops to form a symbol for the building.

His latest "heroic" work, L'Omnibus: A Forum for the Planet, designed for the exhibition "Paris: Architecture and Utopia" (1989), is a meeting place where environmentalists can exchange ideas, methods, and technology. Simultaneously a warning, with its policemanlike "arms," the building can be dismantled, "should we succeed in meeting the challenge facing our society." Parts of it can be removed; the rest will serve as a victory memorial.

6| *L'Omnibus: A Forum for the Planet, Paris. 1989. Collage.*

6|

4 *Horst Korber Sports Center, Berlin. 1990. Roof view with structural elements.*

5 *Sports Center. Roof under construction.*

1 Hafenstrasse Housing
Project, Hamburg, Germany. 1989.
Preliminary painting.

1

ZAHA HADID

2

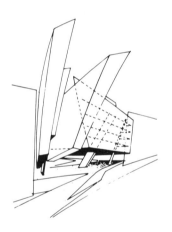

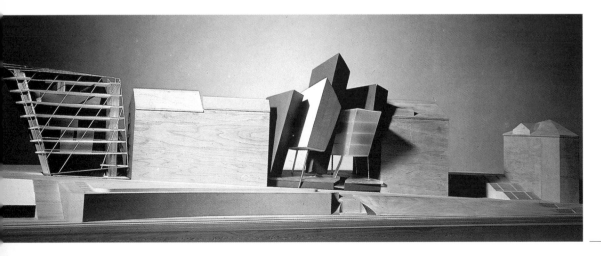

2 Hafenstrasse Housing.
Drawings of preliminary design
for middle site.

3 Hafenstrasse Housing. Model.

3

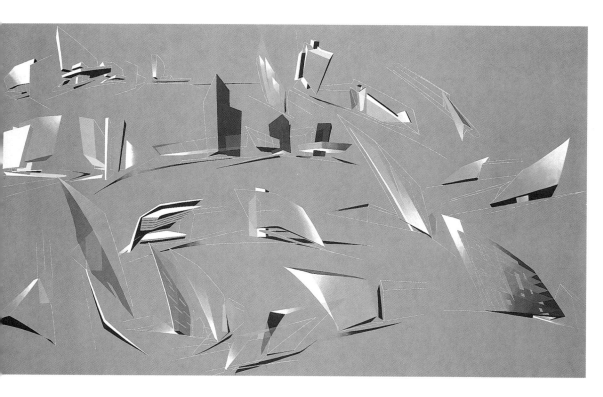

When Zaha Hadid won the competition for The Peak in Hong Kong in 1983, there occurred a major shift in the entire perspective of twentieth-century architecture. There was, of course, a sheer brilliance in the clarity and assuredness of the darting forms, but there was also a tremendous sense of escape from the various dithering machinations that architecture of the 1970s and early 1980s had fallen prey to. Historians will no doubt latch on to the connection between her work and that of OMA (Office for Metropolitan Architecture), of which she was a member, and many have already made much of her knowledge of and predilection for Russian architecture of the 1920s. But all this does is undervalue or even overlook the special quality of Hadid's eye and her talent for placement, which immediately elevate her work above that of her precursors and followers.

One of her analytical and graphic techniques is to draw a set of views of the designed object from a rotating series of distant positions. The dynamic qualities of the form and of her vision are allied. Often the implication of speed of vision carries the observer forward in sheer exhilaration, eliminating the normal process whereby a given position or element is checked for its appropriateness or correctness of juxtaposition.

Any notion that The Peak project was an isolated outburst of talent has long been banished by a continuous stream of powerful designs for buildings. A major step forward was made in her design for a thin "wall" building: a suite of offices on the Kurfürstendamm in Berlin that features a gently folded skin and a deft detachment of the new building from the wall. With this building, Hadid commenced a series of exercises of increasing dexterity and aesthetic fine-tuning. For a project in Tokyo, she developed a program of continuous tucking and folding; for

Zaha Hadid was born in Baghdad, Iraq, in 1950. She studied first at the American University, Beirut, where she received her bachelor's degree in mathematics, then at the AA, from 1972 to 1977, when she was awarded the diploma prize. She taught at the AA from 1977 to 1987. In 1988 she was a visiting design critic at Harvard, and the following year a visiting professor of architecture at Columbia.

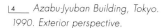

└4___ Azabu-Jyuban Building, Tokyo. 1990. Exterior perspective.

|5___ MoonSoon Restaurant,
Sapporo, Japan. 1990. Interior of Fire
Bar.

7

social housing in another part of Berlin she managed to make her building envelopes virtually "fly" out of the normally constraining urban-block system of that city.

There is a recognizable consistency in the parts of her architecture—clear surfaces, pointed ends, the aforementioned "darts" and "folds"—which are similar to the details of fabric in the hands of a couturier. Also displayed is an innate sense of density and weight, something rarely demonstrated by her numerous imitators.

7 | 8   *MoonSoon Restaurant.
Interior of Ice Bar.*

6   *MoonSoon Restaurant. Exterior
of Fire Bar.*

8

1|

E R I C   O W E N   M O S S

One may be initially attracted or repulsed by the spread-eagled legs or lurching roofs of an Eric Owen Moss building, but eventually one becomes intrigued —even unnerved—by such paradoxes as a space that, while consciously made to express containment, is left with only part of a roof. In Moss's work an ordered sequence of events, which implies a continuous logic, will suddenly be violated, not simply by a politely contrasting series but by something blatantly subversive.

Moss is creative and skilled in achieving the exact degree of imagery he wants. In his recent work—a series of increasingly discursive buildings that use context as a component—his penchant for defining and shocking has become less important than previously. In part, this is by necessity, since they are elaborate remodeling jobs, but they go so much further than other such work; they question the very morality and logic of the building with which they start. The Petal House, for example, is a progression of audacities in which a small house was extended lengthwise, then stretched upward, then straddled. Its pitched roof, which might otherwise be seen as a consummate symbol, is then exploded to the winds—hence the term "petal."

Working with some of the languishing hulks of Culver City, Moss has infiltrated the old movie town in a quizzically heroic manner. The old Paramount Laundry retains much of its composure at first sight, but it is in fact restructured to carry a virtual megastructure within itself. A long pavilion sits alongside the new structure, flanked by "trays," and it can be read from the outside—but only sometimes. Naturally, Moss introduces some icons of his own, such as leaning clay pipes filled with concrete, and cut-out elements, but it is the nonchalance of the thing that counts.

Born in 1943, Eric Owen Moss attended the College of Environmental Design at the University of California, Berkeley, and graduated with honors in 1968. He then attended the Graduate School of Design at Harvard University, receiving his M.Arch. in 1972. He became a professor of design and a member of the board of directors at SCI-ARC in 1974, a post he has held to the present day. In 1976 he opened his own practice. Among the many awards he has received are two for the Petal House, and a recent AIA award for the Central Housing Office Building, 1989.

3 | Paramount Laundry. Third-floor
interior, showing helical stairway with
re-bar handrail.

| 69

4 | _____ Lindblade Tower and Paramount
Laundry. Partial elevation from the
northwest.

5 | Lindblade Tower and Paramount
Laundry. Elevation with fragment of
site plan.

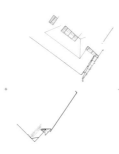

4 |

2 | Lindblade Tower and Paramount
Laundry, Culver City, California.
1989. Interior of laundry.

2 |

5 |

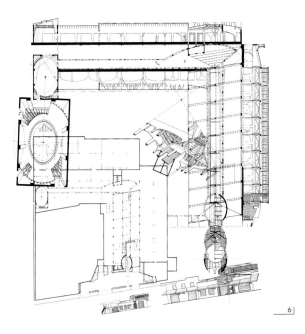

Nearby, at 8522 National Boulevard, Moss has effected a more theatrical or sequential infiltration of five contiguous ware-houses. Sequences, breaks, joints, and truly gothic atmospherics are achieved by a skilled stripping away of skins and surfaces to reveal the skeleton. Within this shell appear some elliptical spaces of a more contemplative quality.

By contrast, the Central Housing Office Building at the University of California's Irvine campus posits a dual objective within a separate and new building. The five constituent elements are externalized as individual outcroppings from an otherwise unified form of roof and base. But, of course, things are not as simple as that, for the substance of the building erodes and the surfaces twist and drop. There is an overall ambiguity of image: the build-ing is a composite of domestic elements on the one hand and disintegrated institutional forms on the other. In many ways, it presents Moss as the manipulator of our referential antennae on a scale that is new for his work—that of the single, heroic object.

⌞9⌟

⌞71⌟

6⌟ *8522 National Boulevard,*
Culver City, California. 1988–90.
Composite drawing.

7⌟ *8522 National Boulevard.*
Entrance ellipse.

8⌟ *8522 National Boulevard.*
Conference room.

⌞9 *8522 National Boulevard.*
Front facade.

⌞10 *Central Housing Office Building,*
University of California, Irvine. 1988.

⌞10

Imre Makovecz's buildings, which often have an exuberant
form and an unexpected combination of surfaces, are difficult

I M R E   M A K O V E C Z to characterize for those brought
up on a simple diet of "hot" or "cold," reactionary or modern.
He is known as a man who embraces the opportunities offered
him, as when he became the architect for a forestry company,
and works effectively with local communities and builders. Yet
he is also highly sophisticated in his use of geometries and
materials.

In his own words, Makovecz's architecture is "an experiment
(not a technical one) to see how, given the established social
conditions, the present power structure, and the shape of our
civilization, and working with my fellow men, I can make the
forgotten, archaic world reappear. The spirit of a place—geo-
logical conditions, remnants of folk art, local materials, vegetation, and the indigenous people—can be the motifs as well as
the motive force of the drama of architecture."

Seeking an archaic world might at first seem to contrast wildly
with the goals of many other architects in this book, but the
built results of this search in fact have much in common with
other contemporary work. It is highly spatial, structurally forceful,
and extremely inventive. The sources of Makovecz's invention
are to be found perhaps equally in traditional Hungary and
in twentieth-century mechanization, and he is clearly more com-
fortable with this duality than some of his fellow architects in
Western Europe. He enjoys the involvement of carpenters and
other craftsmen, letting them extemporize and choose the method
they feel happiest with.

Makovecz acknowledges influences as diverse as Heidegger,
Jung, Steiner, Frank Lloyd Wright, and Celtic mythology and
culture, but more particularly that of the Hungarian philosopher

1| Cultural Center, Sárospatak,
Hungary. 1974/83. Roof detail.

2___ Cultural Center. Main entrance.

4| *Nature Education Center,
Visegrád, Hungary. 1988.*

4|

Bela Hamvas, who was an expert on ancient religions, myths, and beliefs. There is a distinctly religious atmosphere to some of the interiors of Makovecz's buildings: the roofs of the Cultural Center at Jászapáti, the Cultural Center at Sárospatak, and the Nature Education Center at Visegrád follow from his most famous "backbone" roof in the Mortuary Chapel in Budapest of 1977. Trees are used as pillars, grass is encouraged up and onto the tops of buildings. Windows can be Secessionist in both complexity and detail (as in Sárospatak), deadpan (as in the Community Hall at Jászkisér), or orificial (as at Visegrád).

In two current works, the Roman Catholic Church at Paks and the Cultural Center for Szigetvár, Makovecz creates an architecture that is exuberant, but in a hierarchical way. The transition from ground to dome in the Cultural Center is more classically handled than in earlier work, and both buildings display a certain symmetry; these buildings are less organic than his previous ones. But the real key to his work may well be his small constructions for camp facilities and farm buildings, where he is able to achieve a state of knowing *bricolage* similar to the spirit of both Bruce Goff and Frank Gehry.

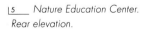
5___ *Nature Education Center.
Rear elevation.*

5___

6| *Roman Catholic Church, Paks, Hungary. 1990. Interior under construction.*

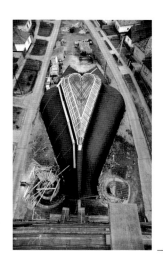

Born in Budapest in 1935, Imre Makovecz studied at the Technical University there and received his diploma in 1959. He worked in the Budapest Town-Planning Office, the Design Office of Cooperatives, and the Design Office for Town Planning, all government organizations. He became the architect for the Pilis Park and Forest Company in 1977 and set up his own practice, Makona, in 1983. He is a member of the Hungarian Association of Architects, an honorary member of the American Institute of Architects, and a member of the International Academy of Architects.

7| *Roman Catholic Church. Towers under construction.*

8| *Roman Catholic Church. Aerial view, under construction.*

KAZUO SHINOHARA

1 | Centennial Anniversary Hall, Tokyo
Institute of Technology. 1988. View
from the north.

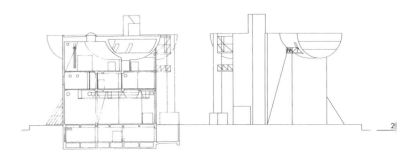

There is a power in the utterances of Shinohara's work that distinguishes it from all other Japanese architecture. Insofar as it concerns itself with issues of values and responses, such discussion has been built up through a concerted, self-referential process. The spareness of Shinohara's objects belies the fact that they have had to deal with as many vicissitudes as befall any other work, but they seem to carry a coherent, developing narrative. The narrative has to do with a set of stated objectives: first, the question of tradition (its frontality, structure, and symbolism); then, questions of pure geometric form, which seem to oppose his earlier concerns.

In his essay "Zero Degree Machine," he writes: "Since I do not believe in the existence of total meaninglessness, I am convinced that a relative value can be achieved from elements that have lost meaning and have been reduced to the zero degree . . . a context in which meaning has been eliminated from symbolic space. . . . My destination is a primary space, a functional space. I have used various adjectives to describe the stages through which I have passed: neutral, inorganic, naked, and so on. . . . Since the late '70s, the machine has been my major theme. . . . The one element that is thought to have rendered modern architecture barren has been a means of visualizing my own ideas about architecture; and although this may seem anachronistic, it is in fact something that has developed autonomously as the direction of my architecture has evolved."

Shinohara's concerns also include the generic quality of the city. With the Centennial Anniversary Hall of the Tokyo Institute of Technology (where he was a professor for many years) he carries through, on a large scale, the connection of "zero degree" parts. He defines the mechanism generating new space

4 *Centennial Anniversary Hall. Interior.*

as "random noise." "Anarchy, or random noise, I hope for as a new vital energy for city and architecture," he says.

It is hardly surprising that the challenge of such ideas, as well as the unnerving quality of the objects themselves, remains a constant reference for the key middle generation of Itsuko Hasegawa (who studied in his research institute), Toyo Ito, and Kazunari Sakamoto, even though their work is necessarily lighter in its chosen language.

5 *Centennial Anniversary Hall. Interior.*

6 |

Kazuo Shinohara was born in
1925 in Shizuoka Prefecture,
Japan. He graduated in 1953
with a degree in architecture from
the Tokyo Institute of Technology,
where for many years following
he was a professor. He was
also a visiting professor at Yale
University and the Technical
University in Vienna. In 1972 he
received the Architectural Institute
of Japan Prize, and in 1988 he
was named an honorary member
of the American Institute of
Architects.

7 | House in Yokohama.

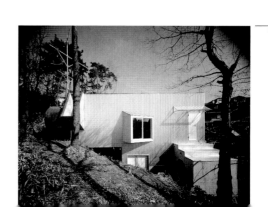

7 |

F O R M A L H A U T

Formalhaut consists of two architects (Gabriela Seifert and Götz Stöckmann) and one sculptor (Ottmar Hörl). Most of their work involves all three partners, and they have taken care to maintain their separate talents: Seifert's lyricism, Stöckmann's astringency, and Hörl's aggressive delight in the world of plastics and commonplace objects.

Hotels designed by Seifert and Stöckmann as their final student projects were quickly followed by an addition to the house of a veterinary surgeon in Gelnhausen. Here a series of varied materials, ranging from blue concrete and sheets of cor-ten steel to layers of customized fiberglass, were inserted into the ground alongside the house. Their more strictly "architectural" work explores such juxtapositions used in "shifting" geometry, though their projects for larger buildings (as yet unrealized) expose another intention: that of the "reduced" building. This can be seen in their proposal for the Anthropological Museum in Frankfurt, where an object resembling a landed space vehicle reveals itself on closer inspection to be a gentle insertion into the parkland.

Their most famous work, the Cow Project, is a commentary on the simultaneous magic, absurdity, offensiveness, and protectiveness of any built object. When the chess game in the project begins, the cows are no longer needed as foils or victims, and the project becomes a comment on the simultaneous magic, absurdity, specificity, and scalelessness of the game-as-city.

It would be wrong, however, to compartmentalize Formalhaut as mere conceptualists or provocateurs, for even their most didactic work reveals a clear interest in substance and aesthetics. It is no accident that the chess game is later reinterpreted as a layout for Houses for Singles and that the subsequent detailing is a precise piece of industrial design. Conversely, their exhibi-

1| 2   *House Extension for a Veterinarian, Gelnhausen, Germany. 1985.*

2

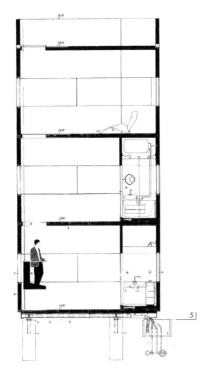

*It is Formalhaut's policy not
to issue biographical details.
The practice is made up of three
partners: Gabriela Seifert, Götz
Stöckmann, and Ottmar Hörl.
The members of the group came
together in 1985 and all live and
work in Frankfurt.*

tion project in Munich, in which a complete caravan is dismembered and arranged in batched piles in a small gallery, displays a continuous love-hate relationship toward the manufactured or controlled object.

The occasional projects where Formalhaut "skins" an existing structure (Oslo, Hamburg, the Frankfurt gravel pits) seem to attack from the inside. They can also be seen as frustrated efforts to re-create the buildings themselves. This is poignant, though, when applied to the gravel-pit workings, unusually organic and nostalgic for a Formalhaut piece, although the skin remains cool and only partially obscurant.

Because Formalhaut is closely associated with the London and Barcelona architectural scenes, its partners enjoy the prospect of "post-technical" architecture. Their work depends on a very good understanding of both the wit of modern technology and the absurdity of much of it. Hörl drops expensive Nikon cameras from high buildings, simultaneously capturing and destroying the extraordinary efforts that created the twentieth-century city and the late-twentieth-century precision instrument.

4 *Double Knight Game, Frankfurt.
1989.*

5 *Houses for Singles. 1988. Section
and plan.*

6|

6| *Rendezvous, Morfelden, Germany.*
1985.

1 Pont des Arts, Paris. 1982.
Drawing.

2 Pont des Arts. Sketch.

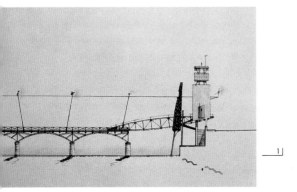

1

3 Bridge Fort, Asperen,
Netherlands. 1989. Sketch.

PETER WILSON

3

4 _ Rosslyn Mews, London. 1988.
Interior.

4

If Peter Wilson had arrived in London by boat, sailing up the
Thames under its many bridges, that might explain his long-
lasting obsession with the two themes that
have inspired much of his work to the present day. But even if
he had he traveled by boat, it would not have been a dug-out
canoe, the shape he has drawn repeatedly, honed, split, and
exploded. And London's prosaic bridges, lacking in ceremony
and celebration, would have held little appeal for him.

One of Wilson's earliest projects was a new bridge across
the Seine in Paris, at the Pont des Arts, springing out from the
embankment of the Académie des Beaux-Arts. It was a deconstructivist work (long before the term was invented), with its
exploded roof and fall-away facades on land, though the actual
bridge, anchored by five boat-shaped pontoons, bore a tough
and practical steel truss. This was followed by his design for
the Accademia Bridge competition at the Venice Biennale. Since
then he has continued to design both bridges and boats, though
now usually for dry, on-land sites.

Wilson was one of a group of inspired tutors at the AA in the
early 1980s, together with Nigel Coates, Zaha Hadid, and
Jenny Lowe. Although he was perhaps the most reclusive of
that group at first, he was highly regarded by students for his
quiet determination, his romanticism, and his intellect. Winning
the competition for the City Library in Münster, Germany, took
him into full-time practice and directed his attention away from
England, but not before he had redesigned the Blackburn House
and rebuilt the interior of his own house and studio in Eaton
Terrace, London. His furniture and interior designs are less well
known—the trick staircases, without handrails, that sometimes
start, disconcertingly, halfway up a wall (the lower steps move
into place only when needed) are characteristic.

5 Rosslyn Mews. Exterior.

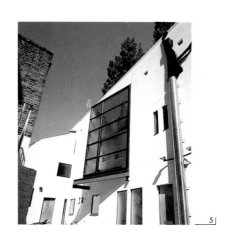

5

6 City Library, Münster, Germany.
1990. Model.

6

7 City Library. Model.

7

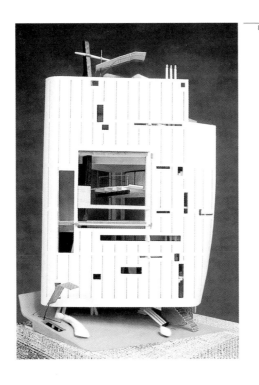

8] *Green Homes Offices, Cosmos Street, Tokyo. 1989. Model of "Structural Ninja."*

Peter Wilson was born in 1950 in Melbourne, Australia, and studied at the local university. He came to England in 1972 to study at the AA and was awarded the diploma prize when he graduated in 1974. For the next four years he worked as an assistant at the school, and in 1978 he ran his own unit in the diploma school. He set up the Wilson Partnership with his wife, Julia Bolles, in 1980; the practice has now become the Architekturbüro Bolles-Wilson to reflect current work in Germany.

The Münster project, conceived as a celebration of the 1,200th anniversary of the founding of the city, was originally to encompass both a library and a museum, but it was later reduced to the library only. The plan was to use the whole site but to make a clear division between the passive elements (the books) and the active (the newspaper room and café). Wilson responded to the altered program with a boat form that was split down the middle from prow to stern, the break forming a passage that aligns with a neighboring medieval church on a strong axis. The perimeter of the building is necessarily disjointed. The books are safe in the strong, encircling curve of the boat, but the public, accessible side is easily penetrated, so that one is directed, by stages, to the core of—and reason for—the library.

An unbuilt scheme, also in Germany, was the Forum of Sand for Berlin, a particularly appropriate idea for the (then) divided city, unstable and segmented. For this Wilson proposed a single-span riveted-steel construction that cut asymmetrically across a segment of the Sand Podium and a "boat with four car-parking towers," a familiar enough shape but enlivened by four vertical "boats" presenting upturned steel-plated keels, anchored to the mother ship by hawsers.

Like Coates and Hadid, Wilson looks to Japan for opportunities. He has recently completed an office design for Green Homes, a media company, on Cosmos Street in Tokyo. The result is a slab building on underground pilotis. At first glance, the structure, with its vertical banding (like newspaper columns) and central cutout square (like a photograph in the middle of the page?), seems to have an obvious, even mundane inspiration; but to those who know his work, it probably resembles the tip of a submarine, just surfacing above the street.

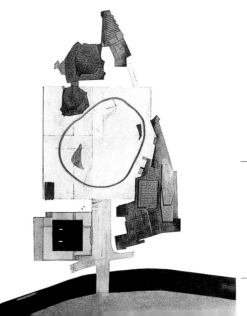

9] *Forum of Sand, Berlin. 1988. Sketch of Sand Podium with bridge.*

GÜNTHER DOMENIG

1 Z-Bank, Favoriten, Vienna. 1979.
Interior.

2⌋ *Z-Bank, Favoriten. Exterior.*

Günther Domenig has discussed the inspiration he has derived from the craggy valleys and mountains of Carinthia, yet he also admits to painstakingly reworking the details of key buildings such as the Z-Bank in Vienna and the Stonehouse he is building for himself in Steindorf.

His formal progress has been evolutionary. After his famous student thesis of a design in the megastructural mode, he completed a series of works (with his former partner, Eilfried Huth) in a variety of styles: brutalist (the Teaching Academy in Graz), formalist (the Parish Center at Oberwart), and mechanistic (the restaurant for the Munich Olympics). In his Convent Hall in Graz the belly of the building explodes into a voluptuous form—strange, perhaps, for a convent.

The story of the creation of the Z-Bank is one of near obsession. The bank has become one of the icons of "informal" architecture of the last ten years, but in fact it depends on a high degree of architectonic control (and even snippets of standardization on the street facade). "The bank was conceived at a time when I finally had the chance to express myself," says Domenig, "notwithstanding its status as a public building. It filled a black hole in the international scene. I am still not free of this building. Perhaps I have transferred a Carinthian mountain landscape to the roof massing of the Z-Bank, which resembles towering mountains. I cannot simply deny all the memories I have from my youth."

More recently Domenig has emerged on several fronts: as a significant teacher and influence (he is the key figure of the Graz School); as the head of an office with several large projects in the works (university buildings and bank headquarters, as well as housing); and as an internationally known architect attached to two powerful pieces of iconography, the bank and the Stonehouse.

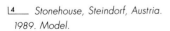 Z-Bank, Zollamtstrasse, Vienna.
1990. Perspective drawing.

4 Stonehouse, Steindorf, Austria.
1989. Model.

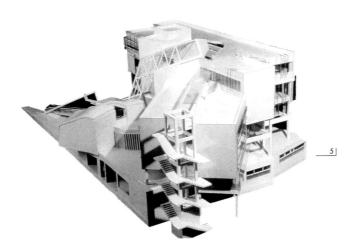

5|

His pursuit of the Stonehouse design is in some ways parallel to the design process for the bank. In plan and section the house is far more aggressive, and in detail it will be more controlled, yet it exhibits a similar obsessiveness. "I inherited the plot from my grandmother," he says. "The project is very much tied up with the places I have lived. To be able to live in a place like this you have to have an independent architecture. That's how I came to do the Stonehouse, which is meant to look like a bank of earth breaking out of the cliffs at the point where the vegetation stops and the cliffs begin and the stone is exposed."

Another thematic development in his work involves the "bird" form. The twisted skins of some of his buildings are revealed, in sketches, to be a direct outgrowth of a series of metal pieces that resemble wings or birds (from book size to several yards long). They appear in built form as canopies, walls, or entryways (as in the Technical University extension in Graz).

Domenig's long and close friendship with Walter Pichler and his friendly, knockabout rivalry with Wolf Prix and Helmut Swiczinsky of Coop Himmelblau provide a clue to the increasing exuberance of his mature period. He has used his status as a regional leader to inspire others, without ever being content with a simple regurgitation of formal tricks. His newest work, honed and sharpened, will no doubt prove even more exciting.

Born in Klagenfurt, Austria, in 1934, Günther Domenig studied at the Technical University in Graz, graduating in 1959. He worked in various offices in Vienna, Linz, and Wuppertal, and for ten years he was in a partnership with Eilfried Huth. Since 1974 he has had his own offices in Klagenfurt, Graz, and Vienna. His first award was for the Ragnitz Project (with Huth), which won the French International Prize for Urbanism and Architecture in 1969. He has been a guest professor in Germany, Austria, and Turkey and since 1980 has been a professor at the Technical University in Graz.

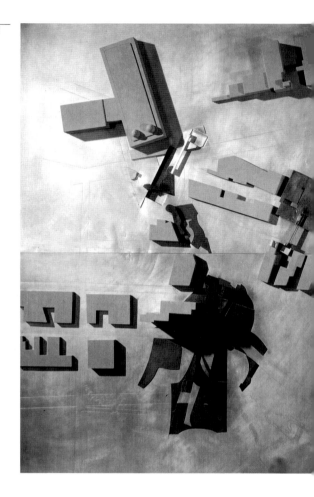

A K S   R U N O Unlike many recent avant-garde architecture firms, Aks Runo (which consists of Bahram Shirdel and Andrew Zago) has focused not on individual buildings but on urbanism, in particular the infilling of parts of the Los Angeles area. Such infill is often radical in profile and topography, but it is always concerned with arriving at a survivable building form.

The Metapolis: Los Angeles project is a typical example. In the architects' own words, "It is a city transformed. It diverges from the history of planning cities that proposes new forms to replace old ones but always operates within the closed framework of forms as discrete, apprehensible objects. The plan of Metapolis is realized through an idea of space envisioned beyond form. Space as place (*topos*) is transformed into space in the making (*chora*). It is the simultaneous occurrence of multitudes of things, separated, without centers, with only beginnings and ends. Each is independent and unrelated to the next in scale, appearance, and orientation. *Chora* is a heterogeneous space created by the occurrences themselves and not a continuum of preexisting space into which things are inserted. The geometry of the space, and the *rune* of the plan, is not a universal geometry. It is a heteronomous, personal geometry that enables us to situate the elements in an open and discontinuous field. The introduction of this geometry separates the project from the context of the existing city and from other Euclidian and modernist strategies of city planning. . . . Each independent element of this project acts as a window to the public life of the Metapolis."

Shirdel's work has its origins in the teachings of Daniel Libeskind (and may therefore be compared with that of Hani Rashid), but it has now achieved a certain compactness and intensification. It is now less dependent on tentacles and armature than are other products of the studio at Cranbrook (where Libeskind

3 La Place Jacques-Cartier,
Montreal. 1990. Aerial view of
model.

Andrew Zago received his B.F.A. from the

University of Michigan and his M.Arch. from

Harvard University's Graduate School of Design.

Since 1986 he has been a faculty member at

SCI-ARC, where he teaches advanced courses in

geometry and architectural drawing.

2 Tokyo International Forum, Tokyo.
1989. Aerial view of model.

4   Olympic West, Los Angeles.
1988. Drawing of Site 1.

5   Olympic West. Model of Site 1.

4

5

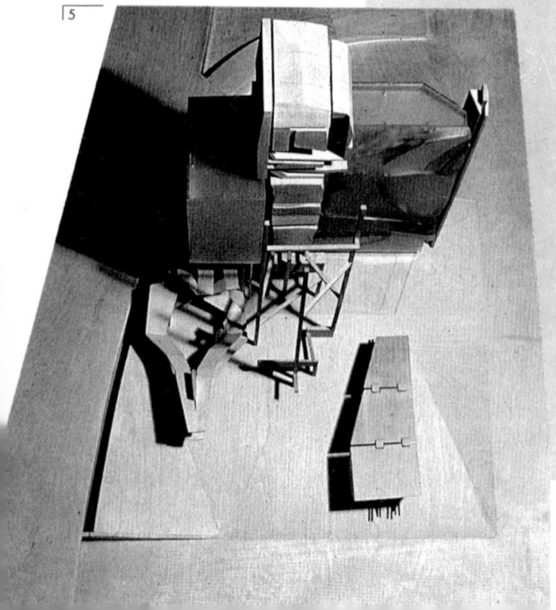

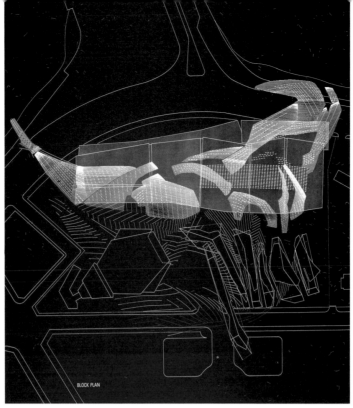

BLOCK PLAN

6 | *Alexandria Library, Alexandria, Egypt. 1989. Drawing.*

Bahram Shirdel received the Christopher Wren Medal from the Royal Institute of Canadian Architects in 1979 and graduated with distinction from the Cranbrook Academy of Art in 1982. He has taught architecture and theory at Harvard University, the University of Houston, and the University of Illinois at Chicago. In 1988 he was coordinator and design instructor for the Architecture Intermundium program in Italy; he is now a senior faculty member at SCI-ARC.

Aks Runo was established in 1987 in Los Angeles.

taught). There is a certain irony, too, in the fact that both Shirdel and Zago are important teachers at SCI-ARC—that most inspired of the Los Angeles architecture schools, where the approach to urban infill is brilliant but loose—yet their method is very much that of consolidation.

In their Olympic West project for West Los Angeles, Aks Runo displays this compactness in both low-rise and high-rise building types; even the serving armatures of the high rise are embraced and controlled. It seems that Shirdel and Zago respond differently when confronted with the more proscribed culture (and more complex program) involved in the Alexandria Library project, where they reveal their considerable formal skills.

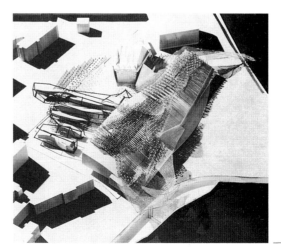

| 7 |

7 | *Alexandria Library. Model.*

E I S E L E + F R I T Z

⌐1 _Saalgasse House, Frankfurt._
1988. Oblique view of facade.

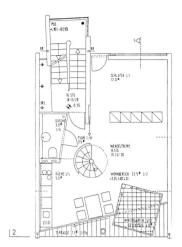

Born in 1948 near Hannover,

Germany, Johann Eisele studied

construction engineering

at the Technische Hochschule in

Darmstadt before moving to archi-

tecture. He worked in the offices of

Emmler & Führer for two years

after graduating. He has taught

design and building construction

at Darmstadt since 1979 and was

a guest professor for a year at the

Bremen College for Art and Music.

Unlike most of their contemporaries in Germany, Johann Eisele and Nicolas Fritz fulfill the potential of a well-funded and well-educated country with a splendid tradition of modern architecture: their work combines an imaginative but not shrill use of twentieth-century technology with a creative but not eccentric conception of space and geometry.

Their larger, more recent work is even more exuberant than their earlier buildings in the Darmstadt area. Their work can be discussed alongside that of the Viennese architects Gerngross and Richter—the former's Kaiser's Café in Darmstadt seems to have a lively dialogue with the latter's Chinese restaurant in Vienna—but Eisele and Fritz's buildings are more controlled in plan.

In their competition project for the Post Museum in Frankfurt there is a normal enough U-plan, with one arm linking into the old villa and a courtyard preserving the old trees, but from there the structure explodes into linking bridges, fractures, and a multitude of cuts into the basic box. At around the same time they were starting to build a house in the rhetorically "architectural" Saalgasse in Frankfurt. A semicircular section of roof falls front-to-back and the house is etched out to the south (street) side and held tight at the back. Within the house is a pair of double volumes, and the barrel-topped space contains an intensification of the structural elements. Their expressionism is direct: steel horizontal bars, glass-brick circulation spaces, and colored framing are used as needed, but never gratuitously.

In 1986 Eisele and Fritz won the competition for the Post Office in Hamburg. Once again, their basic move is to striate the site with a series of parallel lines contained within the natural site boundary. The lines become a planning matrix and a grid for the placement of columns. This system can then be used for boxing out the major functional spaces and dropping the eccentric

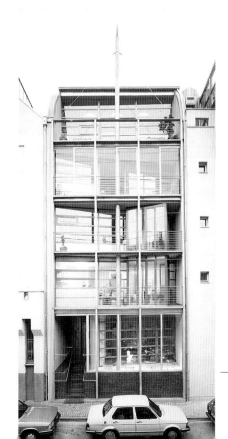

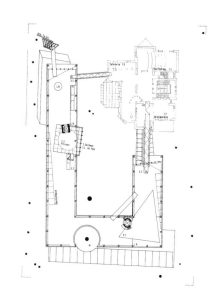

Nicolas Fritz, born in France
in 1948, received his diploma
from the Darmstadt Technische
Hochschule in 1974. For a year he
worked in town planning, and
between 1975 and 1977 he worked
with Georges Candilis on buildings in Austria, Saudi Arabia,
and Lebanon. In 1978 he began
teaching at Darmstadt and
has been a guest professor at the
Bremen College for Art and Music
and the Technical University in
Karlsruhe.

Eisele and Fritz began working
together in 1979.

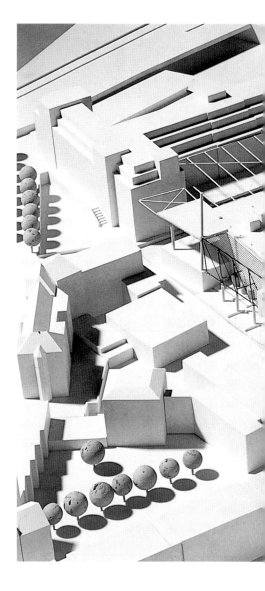

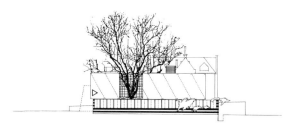

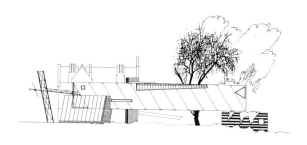

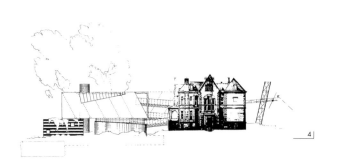

4

objects into the remaining space; the more lyrical path of the perimeter is allowed to have its own quite powerful expression. In this way we get a building within a building and one that is not afraid to enjoy itself. The Post Museum presents a series of wild elements thrusting out of a controlled basic figure, whereas the Post Office reverses the process, holding wild elements to itself in the form of elevational variations.

Their work is reminiscent of several recent Japanese buildings, also the product of a well-informed, technologized culture, which use a straightforward interplay of structural geometry and planning logic with cleverly draped skins and expressionistic tricks. But whereas a Japanese would throw caution to the wind, Eisele and Fritz are circumspect: their little Schrumpf House is inventive in one dimension but very well mannered in others. Their architecture is getting bolder, however, and without resorting to the primacy of imagery that characterizes Japanese work.

4 | *Post Museum, Frankfurt. 1982. Plan
and elevations.*

5 | *Post Office, Hamburg, Germany.
1986. Aerial view of model.*

SZYSZKOWITZ + KOWALSKI

1| *House in Harmisch, Austria. 1988.
View from the village.*

2| *Harmisch House. Facade detail.*

⌊4

The work of Michael Szyszkowitz and Karla Kowalski extends the territory of the Graz School, bringing it back into a direct

confrontation with the traditions of the mountainside architecture of Austria. In some ways their architecture is less urban than that of Günther Domenig (with whom they worked) and less cerebral than that of Volker Giencke. It is largely made up of solid pieces that are twisted and balanced to arrive at unexpectedly delightful results.

The Schloss Pichl is typical: it recalls a traditional compound structure, yet the formal elements are pushed and dragged toward and away from the basic system of the building. The architects also create original alternatives here to conventional window openings, dormers, and clerestories.

In the church complex at Graz-Ragnitz, the development of the actual components becomes much more important. The internal spaces of the church, for example, are unusual but quite controlled. A certain consistency begins to harness (or rationalize) the inventive exuberance of the elements, transforming them into "useful devices." This quality distinguishes the work of Szyszkowitz and Kowalski from that of the expressionist architects in Germany and Holland during the 1920s. It also suggests that Kowalski's training, at the Darmstadt Technische Hochschule during a period when structuralist influences were prevalent, is expressed less in terms of shape or geometry than in terms of conceptual thinking.

Their housing demonstrates skillful planning that integrates small-scale invented parts. It too is reminiscent of de Klerk's work in Amsterdam, but it is developed in an altogether tougher way, creating a memorable environment for family life.

⌐3⌐ *Harmisch House. Interior view, looking toward roof.*

5 ⎿⎯⎯ Church Complex, Graz-Ragnitz,
Austria. 1986. View of main space.

⎯⎯ 6⌐ Church Complex. Overall view.

Michael Szyszkowitz was born

in Graz, Austria, in 1944 and

studied at the Technical University

there. Between 1966 and 1968

he studied urban planning

with Jacob Bakema and Georges

Candilis at the Salzburg

Summer Academies. He worked

for Behnisch & Partner on the

Olympic buildings in Munich

and with Domenig and Huth

in Munich and Graz.

Karla Kowalski was born in
Upper Silesia, Germany, in 1941
and attended the Technische
Hochschule in Darmstadt. After
studying with Georges Candilis in
Paris, she did postgraduate work
at the AA in London and then
worked with Behnisch & Partner
in Munich. She taught for a year
at the Gesamthochschule in Kassel,
and since 1988 she has been
a professor of public building and
planning at Stuttgart University.
Szyszkowitz and Kowalski have
worked together since 1973. They
set up their office in Graz in 1978.

| 8 |

| 7 | Church Complex. Roof detail.

| 8 | Church Complex. Interior, looking
toward entrance.

1____ Hafenstrasse Workshops and
Apartments, Hamburg, Germany.
1989. Model.

ALSOP AND LYALL

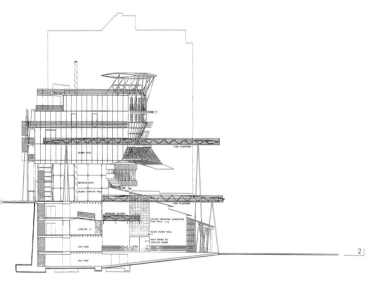

2 | Hafenstrasse Workshops and
Apartments. West elevation.

William Alsop and John Lyall, two British-born architects, have
succeeded in the delicate task of persuading civic authorities in
England and Europe that good
design is not incompatible with public building. Their reputation
grew at first through entries to invited competitions, which eventually led to building opportunities. The sites that they like to
design for are the "difficult" ones: the neglected, run-down areas
of working towns, and especially the dock areas of London and
Hamburg. After a brief flirtation with postmodernism, their work
has become tougher, reflecting these locations—sites whose
raw fabric they attempt to match by exploiting the structural
elements of a building.

The Hafenstrasse Workshops and Apartments were the result
of a commission from the city-planning department of Hamburg.
The site is in an area populated by a community of squatters
who have consistently resisted attempts to revitalize the area.
By building a block of apartments for young families and single
people and providing a variety of small work spaces, the city
hopes that the area can be improved in a way that is acceptable
to its current residents. The building occupies a site between
two busy roads on different levels, another difficult aspect of
the program. Alsop and Lyall's solution was to put the housing
in a separate structure, raised above the higher-level road on
columns and a massive steel truss. The two facades have entirely
different characteristics, one with a patchwork of glazing and
stainless-steel mesh, the other with a steel-plate skin colored
with glass enamel "painting." The top of the building is high-
lighted by a row of airfoil-form shades to protect residents on
the roof terraces from strong sun, wind, and rain.

Their recent work includes a swimming pool at Sheringham,
Norfolk, in the flat and slightly mysterious eastern hinterlands

William Alsop, born in

Northampton, England, in 1947,

trained at the AA in London.

He worked with Maxwell Fry and

Cedric Price in the 1970s, and has

held academic appointments in

Australia, the United States, and

England. He is now a professor at

the College for Art and Music,

Bremen, Germany, and a unit

master at the AA.

4   *Sheringham Leisure Pool,
Norfolk, England. 1988. Interior
view.*

of Britain. The water theme is transmuted here into something soft, almost playful, reflecting the silver light of the sea around the Norfolk coast. One senses that the partners feel at home "north of the Alps," with a colder climate and a brisk, no-nonsense work ethic.

Yet they can also be lighthearted. Their design for the British Pavilion at Expo '92 in Seville (which, sadly, will not be constructed) is a joyful little structure—half spacecraft, half airplane hangar—supported by elongated "spinning-top" columns to one side, with suspended platforms, that seem to be only lightly anchored to the earth. Its sculptural quality reminds us that much of Alsop's work has been with artists, such as Bruce McLean and the sculptor Gareth Jones, with whom he taught for several years.

Thamesmead Town, one of their most recent projects, lies to the east of London, on the site of the former Royal Arsenal, which was built on land reclaimed from the desolate Erith marshes. It is a new town of the 1990s, intended to provide homes for 40,000 people and a full infrastructure of retail, educational, and social facilities. It is the biggest site Alsop and Lyall have built on so far, and initial plans look promising.

5   *Thamesmead Town, London.
1989. Aerial view of model.*

John Lyall was born in Essex, England, in 1949. He has taught at the AA as a unit master and technical tutor. He is a design-panel member of the Cardiff Bay Development Corporation and a committee member of the Royal Institute of British Architects House and Conference Committee.

Alsop and Lyall formed their partnership in 1981.

6   British Pavilion, Expo '92, Seville, Spain. 1989. Model.

6

C H R I S T O P H   M Ä C K L E R

|2| *Computer Animation Laboratory. Entrance hall.*

Christoph Mäckler is one of an ever-increasing band of inventive West German architects who spent a formative period in the office (or, in some cases, the academic studio) of O. M. Ungers. Although to varying degrees their work has edged away from his approach to urban analysis and rational geometry, the younger architects still refer back to Ungers in their recognition of axes and lines of force, in their creation of plazas, and in their subjection of trees, paths, and windows to a participatory role in the overall effect of a city building.

Mäckler's work is an overtly push-pull series of exercises in rationalism on the one hand and expressionistic delight on the other. Much of his work has been concentrated in his home town of Frankfurt, where he has gradually created an interwoven tapestry of monuments, bridges, infills, and arcades. His various competition entries and theoretical projects display his knowledge of and sympathy for the city. Those for the Markthalle, Theaterplatz, and Untermaintor are based on rationalist models, although the last one does have some humor in the way the big blockhouse sits over the historic remnants. In his later Filmpalast Rossmarkt, a combination of movie theaters, offices, and an arcade acts as a spine that bursts out extravagantly at each end.

This practice—allowing a steady element to build confidence and then explode at the end—has become characteristic of Mäckler's major projects. The Schmettering (butterfly) Hochhaus is perhaps the best example. Here the plan takes the outline of the butterfly wings from the site's boundaries (it is located on an island, surrounded by traffic); this remains the only eccentricity in a sixty-story building with strip windows—except, of course, the truly eccentric occurrence of the top butterfly itself.

|4

In a comparatively tall building for the Eschersheimer Landstrasse, a cruciform road intersection is bridged by pairs of legs that join to produce a four-part tower, which is then tickled by a pair of trusslike curved legs and a pair of straight trusses that emanate from blockhouses down the street. A gymnastic display of apparatus, this structure is made up of predictable parts but takes greater risks than the earlier work. Both towers look forward to his later Berlin-Breischeidplatz tower, where the sweeping steel arm thrusts through the top of the solid tower and up to the radio dish.

The simultaneous and contrary influences of rationalism and expressionism can also be seen in his two bridges for Frankfurt: the Alte Brücke contains several Krieresque houses (though the largest one seems to draw on historical precedent), whereas the Holbeinstag, a bridge designed for a new crossing point on the river, celebrates itself with two wing buildings that are clearly inspired by the image of two fish staring at each other.

The detailing of his built work—in such cases as the Computer Animation Library office interior—suggests a third direction in what might be called Viennese formalism: a tactic of resolution, which Hans Hollein (and even Günther Domenig in his "university" style) has used to good effect.

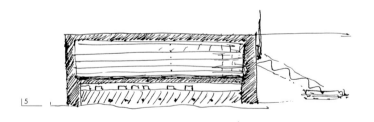
|5

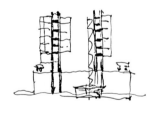

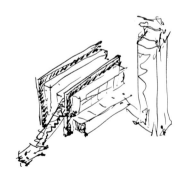

|5___ *German Federal Railway*
Administration Building, Berlin. 1986.
Sketches.

Born in Frankfurt in 1951, Christoph Mäckler studied architecture at the Fachhochschule in Darmstadt. In 1975 he spent a year working with O. M. Ungers in Cologne before continuing his studies at the Rheinisch-Westfälische Technische Hochschule in Aachen. He received the Schinkel Award for the best architectural "newcomer," which allowed him to spend eight months in the United States. He joined his father's architecture firm briefly; by 1981 he had set up on his own in Frankfurt. Since then he has become a visiting professor in Kassel and a member of the Bund Deutscher Architekten.

|6|___ Multistory "Skyscraper." Model.

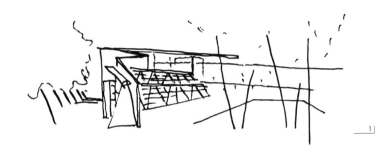

MIRALLES AND PINÓS

Enric Miralles was born in

Barcelona in 1955. After three

years at the Center for Palladian

Studies in Vicenza, he worked

with Piñón and Viaplana and

received his degree in architecture

in 1978. He was a visiting scholar

at Columbia University in 1980–81.

He received his Ph.D. in architec-

ture in 1988.

The meteoric rise in recognition for the husband-and-wife part-nership of Enric Miralles and Carme Pinós is completely justified by their output, which is prodigious and exuberant, yet beautifully controlled when built and spare and discriminating in drawings. Each project seems to move forward from the previous one, and their talent at placement is constantly tested by the audacity with which they thrust out elements, scatter geometries, and—in their most recent work—add witty bits and pieces.

Miralles's experience as a young assistant of Helio Piñón and Albert Viaplana was clearly a base for much of the architecture. This can be seen in the progression from the Plaza de la Estacion de Sants, in which he was involved with Piñón and Viaplana, to the Plaza Mayor, where four years later, working on his own, he created architecture that was wilder, more gawky, but also tougher. A connection can be sensed later, too, between a ceme-tery by Piñón and Viaplana and one planned for Igualada by Miralles and Pinós. The sweeping paths and the linearity are common to both overall schemes, but Miralles and Pinós then developed the buildings in a more technically intriguing manner.

The first building elements to truly express their zeal are those in the conversion of La Lluana factory into a school at Badelona, in 1987. Their additions are elegant but also naughty: stairs that run into ramps, jutting balconies, and a delicious curving, rolling metal entrance door. For the Confederation of Commerce they propose an even more aggressively audacious scheme, where the fourteenth-century Gothic building is juxtaposed with hanging decks on different axes and jagged strips above—an unusual but, in the end, appropriately scaled set of elements.

The idea of partially underground buildings, as well as the point at which the building thrusts out into view, has fascinated

Carme Pinós was also born in Barcelona, in 1954. She worked in the studio of Alberto Noguerol and studied at the International Laboratory of Architecture and Urban Design in Urbino. She qualified as an architect in 1979, studied for a year at Columbia University, and did postgraduate work in urbanism with Manuel Sola Morales.

In 1983 Miralles and Pinós set up their own office, and the same year the couple won the first of many prizes, for their design of a building in the Plaza Mayor in Alcaniz, Spain.

4   5   *Sunshade roofs, Plaza Mayor, Parets del Valles, Barcelona. 1985.*

5

many twentieth-century architects. The Social Center at Hostalets
will surely become a classic of the genre. The cascading, splayed
terraces are countered by staircase cuts. Meeting rooms are
tucked into the hillside. Great steel struts articulate the exposed
sides of the building in a manner that might seem shocking in a
modest town, yet the result is somehow cohesive, in the same
way that the bold elements in the school and the Plaza Mayor
seem to be absorbed.

As their architecture unfolds, we may be able to identify their
vocabulary of devices, but at this point the restlessness of their
work is an outgrowth of the restlessness of their search. Miralles
and Pinós's aspirations seem to be continually daring them to
go further. In the detailing, too, one can see a delight in com-
bining elements that elsewhere would be categorized as high
tech but in their work are used with the same knowing nonchalance that Chareau displayed in his Maison de Verre. Yet unlike
English or American technical architects, Miralles and Pinós have
a distinct regard for solidity, for the nudging and coaxing of
old walls, for the juxtaposition of a staid element with a seemingly darting or floating one. The effect of their work is as if
the craftsmen of Catalonia had absorbed high-grade steel into
their vernacular.

6 _____ Cemetery, Igualada, Spain.
1990. General plan.

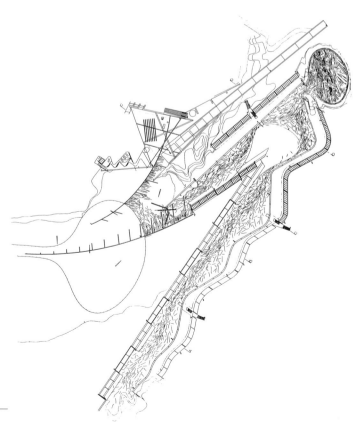

6

1 Benedek House, Graz, Austria.
1986. Detail of north facade.

Born in Carinthia, Austria,

in 1947, Volker Giencke studied

architecture and philosophy in

Graz and Vienna. From 1966

to 1974 he worked for various

architects in Geneva, Munich,

Cologne, Berlin, and Graz, and

in 1979 he set up his own office

in Graz. The same year he was

awarded a scholarship from the

Art Academy of Berlin for research

in the Scharoun archives.

Since 1983 he has taught at the

Technical University, Graz.

He was awarded a prize by the

Association of Austrian

Architecture in 1987 and the

following year won the Styrian

Architecture Prize.

"This is exactly what I like about his architecture: there is always this easiness behind it. Things are so uncomplicated.

V O L K E R   G I E N C K E They become more clear, almost transparent, musiclike." (*Beva-Liisa Pelkonen*)

Volker Giencke has designed and built almost exclusively in and around Graz, Austria, where he has been living for more than a decade. His familiarity with and affection for the town are obvious in his attention to detail and in his response to context: to the harmony of familiar streets, to the beauty of the green hills beyond. But he is not a vernacular architect.

The apparent softness of the Benedek House, with its "ecological" roof covered with earth, grasses, and wildflowers, conceals within its curved facade a surprisingly complex spatial configuration. Set into the gentle slope of a meadow, the ground-floor rooms at the rear lead into a semibasement below the main entrance. The convex facade (concave from within) turns the viewer toward the core of the house, with its stairs and hearth. The children's room is an adjunct, a smaller semidetached bay sensibly leading to a covered veranda. On the exterior, the butterflylike roof, held above the walls by delicate steel struts, soars as though in acknowledgment of the view beyond. The house is timber-framed, with large glazed bays that play with the idea of inside-outside and form a taut skin that wraps around the building. This construction seems to be a more instinctive reaction to a hilly setting than that of the later Reischl House, which uses similar elements but produces a more rigid structure.

The idea of partly concealed, partly revealed space is also present in the Maxonus Shop in Graz. Unable to tamper with the existing facade, which consists of a structural concrete wall with narrow openings and horizontal louvered security shutters, Giencke cleverly put a glass box in front of the entire facade.

2   Benedek House.
West elevation.

3 | Maxonus Shop, Graz, Austria.
1985. Interior.

4

4   *Maxonus Shop. Exterior.*

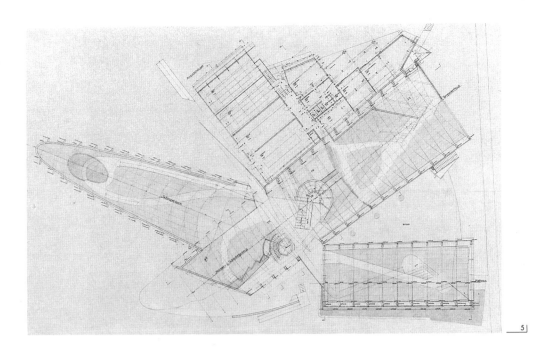

5

The shutters are thus spotlighted; they are at once screened and visible. Diagonally arranged furniture and fittings inside the shop continue the illusion of veiled space.

The new Botanical Gardens of Graz, now under construction, look like the product of a major air disaster. Parts of the aircraft —the wings and the fuselage—have become detached and are lying at acute angles to each other. An unidentified ramp of four steps has been embedded in the shallow hillside. The skin of the aircraft has disappeared; only the skeleton remains. If it is not evocative of a plane, then it looks like some winged insect in serious trouble. Why this particular analogy was chosen is not clear, but it is a powerful image. One wing tip, gouged into the sloping site, forms the subtropical house; another, separated tip forms the cold house. The main body is for cacti and temperate plants, the "steps" for plant nurseries, and an adjacent, hidden level for services. Within the framework are spiral staircases, connecting walkways, and paths that will wind through roof-high trees and around ponds. The arched struts will be the site for tropical creepers, the glazed cages for exotic birds. The whole concept is astonishingly rich in imagery. Giencke's scheme is no exception to the inventive design seen in such glass-house precedents as Kew Gardens in London and Paxton's Crystal Palace.

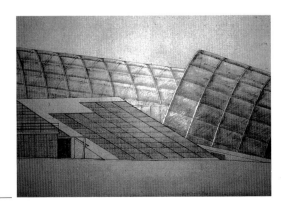

6

6 Botanical Gardens. Elevation.

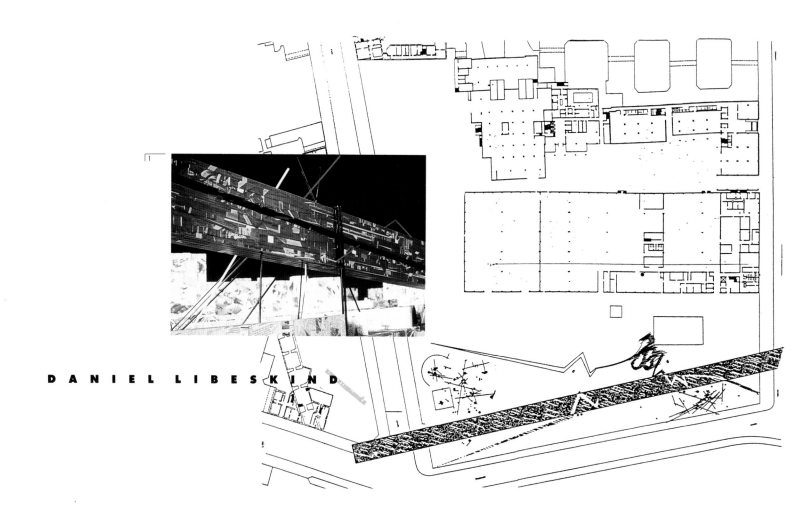

D A N I E L   L I B E S K I N D

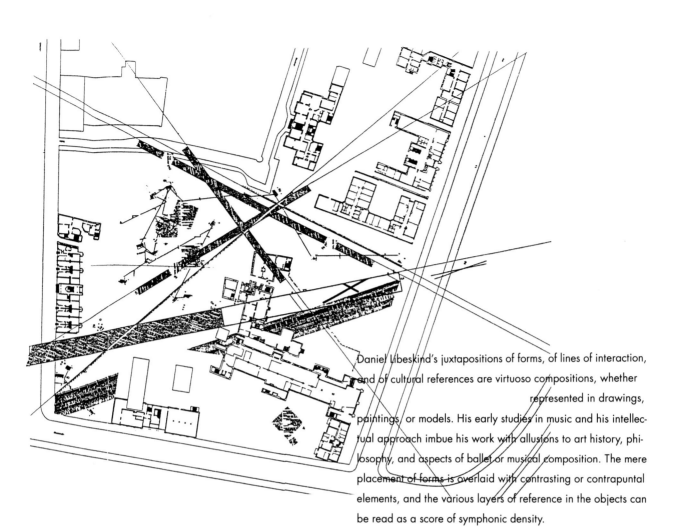

Daniel Libeskind's juxtapositions of forms, of lines of interaction, and of cultural references are virtuoso compositions, whether represented in drawings, paintings, or models. His early studies in music and his intellectual approach imbue his work with allusions to art history, philosophy, and aspects of ballet or musical composition. The mere placement of forms is overlaid with contrasting or contrapuntal elements, and the various layers of reference in the objects can be read as a score of symphonic density.

A student of John Hejduk's at Cooper Union, Libeskind took Cubism as a point of departure in his early work. But by the time of his well-known drawings called "Chamberworks" (first exhibited in 1983), the architectural and formal influences had been scattered to such an extent that Libeskind appeared to be not only inventing a new compositional program but challenging the need for architecture in the first place.

In his contribution to the Venice Biennale of 1985, however, he reconvened some of the fragments in order to create machines: a reading machine, a writing machine, and a memory machine. The memory machine, for example, is dedicated to Erasmus and "refers to Camillo's Memory Theater. . . . Like a Renaissance workshop, it is a revelation of objects suspended by tackles and cord. All the instruments of architecture can be found here and have been put to use. When the machine revolves, it makes a clicking sound. . . . As a mechanism of projection and illusion it seeks to disengage—as a ghost of Humanism's cosmic hubris —the ten themes of the Biennale from locations where they are placed in order to return them to their original destined locus: James Joyce's Dublin and Tatlin's Moscow. The memory machine contains eighteen subordinate spectacles, among them the 'cloud machine' and the 'wave machine,' as well as the 'schizo-

2 |

4

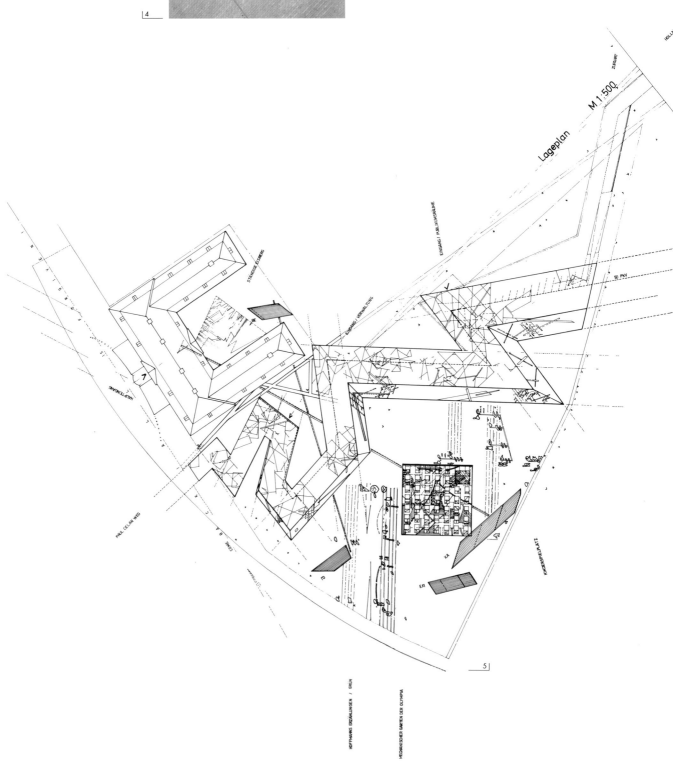

5

phrenic forum.'" Libeskind's description makes clear the conceptual inspiration behind his constructed work. This approach has had a great influence on many young architects who became aware of Libeskind's work as his reputation as a teacher and lecturer grew worldwide by the mid-1980s.

His recent developments have been heroic. In 1987 he won the first prize in the last city-planning competition of Berlin's IBA series with a giant inclined slab linked to Flottwellstrasse by a triangular composition of thin strips of building. The details of this scheme are a refinement of the architecture of the "machines."

Two years later, he won first prize for the extension of the Berlin Museum (to house its Jewish department, among other things). Here the diagrammatic dynamics and the richness of objects and references are harnessed to a dramatically conceived program of exhibition spaces. The outside space, too, becomes a brilliant tabula rasa into which the built solids are thrust. As in the case of Bernard Tschumi, Libeskind has shown that a "conceptual" or academic architect of considerable influence (but regarded by the public as a "paper" architect) can eventually outshine many worthy talents in open competition.

Daniel Libeskind was born in 1946 in Poland, studied music in Israel, and received his B.Arch. from Cooper Union in New York and his M.A. in the history and theory of architecture at Essex University in England. He was head of the department of architecture at Cranbrook Academy of Art and has taught at Harvard's Graduate School of Design, the Danish Academy of Art in Copenhagen, the University of Naples in Italy, and other schools. He was the founder and director of Architecture Intermundium in Milan and was one of seven architects featured in the 1988 "Deconstructivist Architecture" exhibition at New York's Museum of Modern Art.

5| *Berlin Museum Extension. Site plan.*

6| *Memory Machine, Venice Biennale. 1985.*

Team Zoo is a loose consortium of architects, designers, plan-
ners, and other artists tied together by the philosophy of the

T E A M   Z O O late Takamasa Yoshizaka. His theories involved a cautious
attitude toward modernism, a rebellion against restrictions, and
an insistence on the freedom of the individual human being. The
members of Team Zoo are divided into cells or ateliers named
after animals: *zo* (elephant), *iruha* (dolphin), *kuma* (bear), *wani*
(crocodile), *gali* (ox).

The plans of Team Zoo's small buildings can be quite romantic;
in the case of the Domo Serakanto of 1974, the plan anticipated
European deconstructivism of the 1980s. The interior displays
a fairly uninhibited conglomeration of surfaces and forms; the
building as a whole takes on the iconography of a fish—with
gills, spine, teeth, and scales. The critic Mayumi Miyawaki has
commented that "the eyes of Team Zoo are trained on the world
of handicraft . . . their greatest strength and greatest peril. . . .
The danger is that they will be swallowed up by sentiment."

More noticeable in their later—and larger-scale—work is
a basically classical approach to the plan. In the Miyashiro
Community Center of 1980, the plan is a centrifugal composition
that suddenly erupts into quite voluptuous or vegetational lines.
The major elements are equally surprising, with some parts
recalling the early structural modernism of Auguste Perret and
others evoking a ruined amphitheater and still others taking the
form of assertive rows of spiked pylons. It is said that on their
drawings Zoo members often sketch banyan trees, a symbol
of the vitality of Okinawa (their home). Many of the words they
use attempt to express the world of forms—*giza-giza* (jagged,
latticed, or notched), *dandan* (stepped, graduated, rounded)—
and the ambiguous curves of the building themselves come
from the flora of Okinawa. The compounding of these forms

2| |3   4| *Shinshukan Community Center, Miyashiro, Japan. 1980.*

2|

4|

with the overlay of concentric circles, radiating lines, and grids in the community center creates special conditions of light and shadow, a theatrical effect.

They write of themselves: "It is our aim to create harmony between architecture and the environment. For that purpose, we apply *aimai moku* and *jiku*. *Aimai moku* implies that which is undefined, vague, or ambiguous. An *aimai moku* space is by nature multifunctional and able to evoke various responses and moods. Such space serves to stimulate the imagination with a feeling that is boundless, free-flowing, and peaceful. To erase the division of inside and outside, for example, we provide *aimai moku* spaces as areas of transition: porches, verandas, platforms, eaves, pilotis, open colonnades, and arbors generate continuity in passing from outside to inside without an abrupt change of atmosphere. . . . People can meet here in their comings and goings and are provided with greater opportunities for communication. This is the 'hand-shaking' point between the building and the community. We also apply the traditional concept of *jiku*, which means axis. By using points of reference found in the natural landscape, the physical organization of the local town, celestial bodies, or the changing seasons, we establish axes that converge on the site. From the layering of these axes we select the orientation and capture the dynamic flow of the landscape and the cosmos. The axes focus energy into the structure. Once we are inside the building, our imaginations are propelled along the axes outward. . . . Finally, the greening of the space with vegetation is most important."

A typical approach is seen in the Yoga Promenade of 1986, where the rehabilitation of an old street becomes the frame for a series of streams, seats, humps, and bridges. The design is strangely reminiscent of a traditional Japanese woodcut of village life and at the same time unfettered and inventive.

7 | *Yoga Promenade, Tokyo. 1986.*
Detail.

Hiroyasu Higuchi was born

in Shizuoka, Japan, in 1939 and

studied at Waseda University.

Reiko Tomita was born in 1938

in Tokyo and studied at Tokyo

University. Other members of

Team Zoo, which was founded in

1971, are Y. H. Chen, Kenji Hojo,

Erai Iwata, Tomono Iwata,

Ichiro Machiyama, Tamegoro

Nagata, Masahiro Nishio, Masako

Nunokawa, Shigeru Sakamoto,

Takaaki Sato, Ikuyo Seki, Satoshi

Tanada, Monchen Tsai, and

Mandy Winford.

7 |

FRANK GEHRY

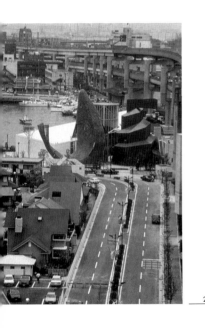

1 Fishdance Restaurant, Kobe, Japan. 1986. Exterior view.

2 Fishdance Restaurant. View of the buildings in context.

3 Fishdance Restaurant. Interior.

"I am interested in finishing work, but I am interested in the work's not appearing finished, with every hair in place, every piece of furniture in its spot ready for photographs. I prefer the sketch quality, the tentativeness . . . rather than the presumption of total resolution and finality." It is this quality of "unfinishedness," not to be confused with irresolution, that characterizes Gehry's best work. He has been criticized in the past for using cheap materials like corrugated-metal panels, chain-link fence, and mesh in an effort to keep within limited budgets. But in his search for cut-rate solutions, he has developed a particular style that could be described as "expedient architecture," making a virtue out of necessity.

The eclectic buildings of Los Angeles—buildings that can mimic practically anything, from beach architecture to full-blown Spanish colonial—have provided a source of inspiration, a rich contextual background. Gehry's Norton Residence in Venice, California, built for a screenwriter, has a detached study overlooking the beach that was inspired by nearby lifeguard stations and an adjacent apartment building; it forms a powerful compositional element when viewed from the house.

A strong sculptural sensibility runs through Gehry's work (he has collaborated with Claes Oldenburg, Anthony Caro, and Donald Judd). "I approach each building as a sculptural object, a spatial container, a space with light and air. The manipulation of the inside of the container is for me an independent sculptural problem and no less interesting than the design of the container itself." The Fishdance Restaurant in Kobe, Japan, takes this idea to extremes. For the site, located on a busy waterfront, with shipyards, cranes, and docks, Gehry designed three freestanding objects: a copper-clad spiral form that houses a bar and tempura counter; a sloped-roof building with a clerestory tower

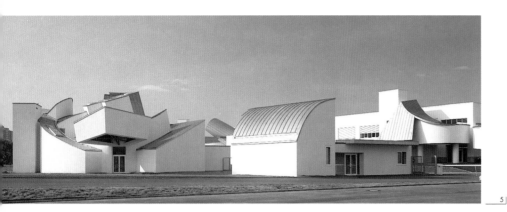

5|

6| *Vitra Museum. Gallery space.*

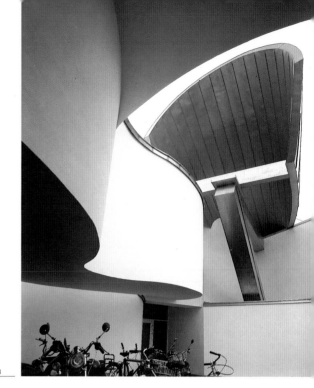

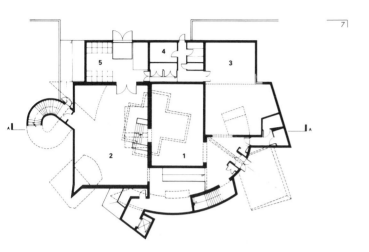

7|

for the kitchen and main dining area; and an extraordinary fish sculpture of chain-link mesh that rears up several stories high.

Another project, the Vitra Factory and Museum in Weil am Rhein, Germany, also contains three elements: an assembly plant; a small furniture museum; and a master plan, with a new entrance road and gatehouse, that allows for future expansion of the factory. Here the ramps and entrance canopies that flank the factory facade make sculptural bookends to the museum. The galleries are treated as connected volumes that spatially inter-penetrate each other, so that exhibitions can communicate from one space to another. Each has a different character, created by volume, surface, scale, and natural light, which is diffused through skylights. The construction is plaster over masonry on vertical surfaces, with metal roofing panels on sloped, water-shedding surfaces. Gehry's training in eclecticism has produced here a stimulating, satisfying building that cannot be slotted into any current category.

8|

|131

Born in Toronto, Canada, in 1929, Frank O. Gehry moved to the United States when he was seventeen. He studied at USC in Los Angeles and at Harvard's Graduate School of Design. He served in the Special Services Division of the U.S. Army in 1955-56. After working in architects' offices in Atlanta, Boston, and Los Angeles, he spent a year in Paris with André Remondet in 1961. He set up his own firm in 1962. He has taught at USC, UCLA, Yale, and Harvard. He is the recipient of numerous awards, including the 1989 Pritzker Prize.

6|

1 — *Steel Cloud, West Coast Gateway, Los Angeles. 1988–91. Detail of model, showing ground-level view.*

2 — *Steel Cloud. Model, showing long view of galleries and libraries above the freeway.*

A S Y M P T O T E

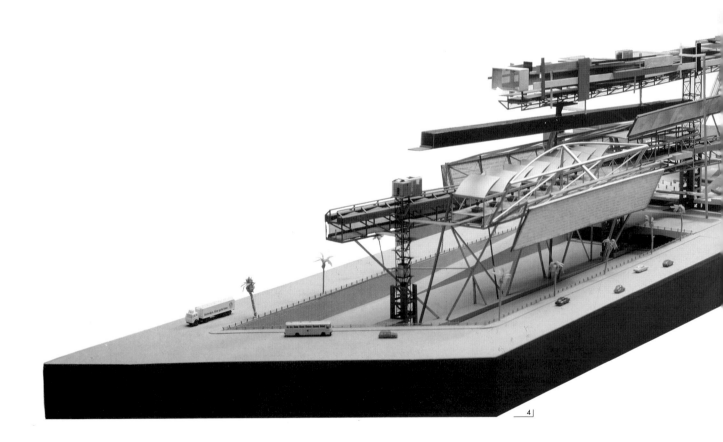

Hani Rashid was born in Cairo, Egypt, in 1958. He received his B.Arch. from Carleton University in Canada and his M.Arch. from the Cranbrook Academy of Art under the direction of Daniel Libeskind. Rashid is currently a visiting professor of architecture at the Columbia University Graduate School of Architecture, Planning, and Preservation.

3   *Steel Cloud. Detail of model, showing winged cinema screens and cinema seating on tracks.*

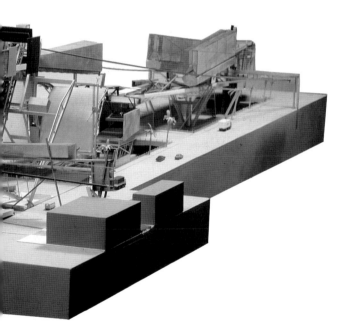

4 | *Steel Cloud. Model.*

When the City of Los Angeles appointed a committee in 1988 to select a monument to commemorate its many immigrants, the resulting competition attracted two hundred entries. A panel of fourteen jurors chose a radical scheme by the little-known partnership Asymptote (Hani Rashid and LiseAnne Couture). Their proposal was to erect a 1,600-foot linear structure directly above the Hollywood Freeway, the main "gateway" to the city. Named Steel Cloud, the project attracted enormous publicity, most of it favorable. One surprise was that the entire structure would be privately financed; another was that a work of such technical virtuousity and soaring imagination should come from two people who had yet to build anything and whose work was unknown to all but a small group of cognoscenti. The previous year Asymptote had produced a major proposal for the Italian city of Lanciano, which, though not implemented, gave many clues that a new talent was at work.

Their projects demonstrate the partners' belief that architecture has reached a critical point where theoretical work, formerly confined to the drawing board, can now be realized. Using "technique" and "sources (memory)," they are exploring uncharted territory, creating mirages of what might be. But, at the same time, they appreciate that the very act of building changes the drawn project.

Steel Cloud has been variously described as the West Coast's answer to the Statue of Liberty (in its role as a landmark structure) and as Daniel Libeskind's notation drawings translated into action. While Libeskind's influence is acknowledged, the proposed structure is an original attempt to promote a linear, not vertical, monument, perfectly adapted to its context. It is described by its architects as "an assembly of horizons lifted and incising the skyline . . . to manifest the metaphysical space

that exists over the interminable freeways of Los Angeles." Steel Cloud incorporates museums, libraries, theaters, and restaurants, enormous screens for video and film projects, a pair of aquariums with sea life from both the Atlantic and the Pacific, and a "musical forest" of electronic synthesizers, all linked by a free-form pedestrian walkway.

Lebbeus Woods, who drew some of the interiors and details, describes it as presenting "two powerful sets of forces: those of the freeway and those of the neighboring streets, ending now at the freeway's edges. Its design crystallizes the public movement there by foot and by car, giving it a broken, staccato form that is something of a tectonic dance, with both pauses and crescendos overlaid, one on the other, in complex, stave-like layers. It is a lyrical image of urban life."

On the other side of the world, in Egypt, Asymptote has produced an equally inspiring and appropriate proposal for the new library in Alexandria, on the Mediterranean coast. Rashid was born in Cairo, south of Alexandria, and the scheme draws on the imagery of the tombs and monuments of the Pharaohs, "submerged into an etherlike landscape of stone and water. The library and its accompanying pavilions were envisioned as a terrain of sleeping gods, alert but shackled, who entrap the spaces used by visitors to the site." The nodal point of these blocks and planes is the Tomb of Books, a seven-story-high tower encased in alabaster, which allows the Egyptian sun to penetrate and "bathe the books in an amber glow." Anathema to librarians, the scheme nevertheless placed third in an international competition—recognition of the architects who are in the forefront of translating sophisticated yet romantic theories into reality.

LiseAnne Couture was born

in Montreal, Canada, in 1959.

She received her B. Arch. from

Carleton University in Canada

and her M. Arch. from Yale

University, and is currently a

professor in the Graduate School

of Architecture at Parsons School

of Design.

7 |

8 |

| 6 | 7 | 8 | *Alexandria Library,*
Alexandria, Egypt. 1989. Views of
model.

In 1986, partners Rashid and

Couture established Asymptote

in Milan as an alternative to the

conventional architectural office.

The studio is now located in

New York.

W O O D / M A R S H

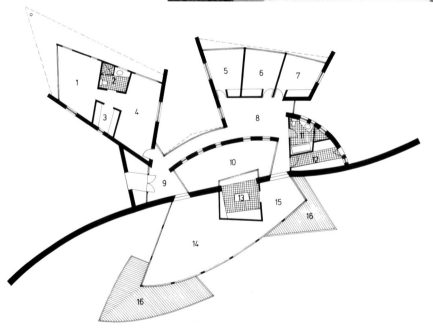

|1___ Choong House, Eltham,
Australia. 1985. Plan.

__2| Choong House. Exterior.

|3 ‾ Choong House. Interior
courtyard.

Behind Melbourne's apparent endlessness and its Victorian
or Edwardian feel is an energy, a creativity, that stems from
its large Greek, Italian, and Balkan popula-
tion. This quality is surely what has made it a far more radical
place than the larger (and more American-seeming) Sydney,
and a more appropriate city for the making of films, books,
and paintings.

From such a setting, and more specifically from the context of
the Royal Melbourne Institute of Technology—Australia's most
intellectually demanding architecture school—there emerged
a group of students, including Roger Wood and Randal Marsh,
who called themselves Biltmoderne. Even before they had
graduated, they were designing and constructing furniture and
nightclubs. Their work was often wild, and its formal and tactile
properties sometimes seemed to be a collage of every risqué
idea imaginable; it always had more than the usual wit.

On a narrow street, they made a few small rooms for the
Macrae & Way film company into something of a permanent,
mechanized set. A barnlike roof with deckled aluminum gables
evoked the same kind of surprise that one experienced in
the narrow streets of Venice, California, when confronted by
the early Morphosis houses. Given a broader canvas in the
Choong House, Biltmoderne produced an inhabitable sculpture
piece that establishes a great climbing spine wall and then enjoys
a series of cuts and thrusts by which the rooms themselves
spread *through* it and *from* it.

Re-forming as Wood/Marsh, the office seems to have continued
its intensification of mode—and discrimination. The Frantzeskos
House extensions wrap, tuck, and fly into and out of the existing house structure and make a knowing sideways reference
to the aesthetic of Frank Lloyd Wright with the leaning chimney

4 Frantzeskos House, Eaglemont,
Australia. 1983. Exterior.

5 Frantzeskos House. West and
north elevations.

4

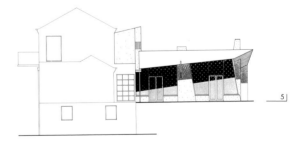

5

6

and roof—an especially piquant allusion, since the house is on an estate planned by Walter Burley Griffin, that most exotic of Wright's collaborators.

The Babic House uses the freedom of an open, coastal site to play out some fundamental propositions. In the designers' own words, the aluminum superstructure is "a suspended carriage that hovers above the landscape with an adjusted perspective. As the land falls away, the building is propped on a massive curved red wall that chops into the terrain and indicates the entry." The instincts here are again part Wrightian and are refreshingly unencumbered by the need to use aluminum as an excuse for the quotational rediscovery of the Australian outback shed (currently a common pursuit).

After graduating from the Royal Melbourne Institute of Technology and working in architectural offices in Melbourne, Roger Wood and Randal Marsh were founding directors of Biltmoderne in 1983. In 1987 they formed Wood/Marsh Architecture. Both Wood and Marsh have been involved at committee level with the Royal Australian Institute of Architecture and have worked with public-arts organizations.

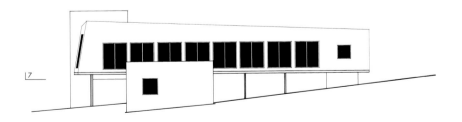

7

1

In the late 1970s news of a very original house designed
by a young architect in the Transvaal, South Africa, filtered
S T A N L E Y   S A I T O W I T Z through to Europe
and America. As was soon revealed in presentations by Stanley
Saitowitz, its architect, the shedlike components of the house,
made from modest materials typical of agricultural structures,
were running over skillfully contrived geometries. A forerunner
of—or perhaps an inspiration for—the explosion of bent and
rolling roofs that subsequently filled student drawing boards in
London and elsewhere, this house was later matched by a second
in the Transvaal. Equally direct and spare, this one was based
on cubic volumes. The early house, published in *Archetype* (a
brilliant but short-lived San Francisco journal), remains a classic
of architectural imagery.

Appointed a professor at the University of California, Berkeley,
in the early 1980s, Saitowitz became one of the leaders (along
with Mark Mack) in the revival of architectural debate in the Bay
Area. His first American projects seemed to rely on a certain
solidity and allusive imagery, but the more recent work has cast
these aside, regaining the freshness and brilliance of line seen
in the early, South African work.

The Grewal House uses a repeated "sweep" gesture and is bold
in its inclusion of such things as acute corners, canted sides,
and a single great roll of roof. The McDonald House inverts the
single-sweep roof and detaches it from the body of the house,
but other characteristic Saitowitz features are here—the canting,
the sweep-and-corner plan. As in the South African work,
a delightfully obvious detailing (which is difficult to do) keeps
the building at the correct scale. Saitowitz is clearly excited by
the location: "The roof: a wave reflecting the nearby ocean.
The space: a cave, carved by water. . . . Shell-like, the outside is

2

3 | Grewal House, Oakland, California. 1987. Section and elevations.

_4____ Grewal House. Model._

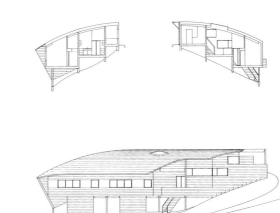

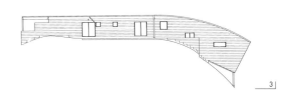

3 |

4

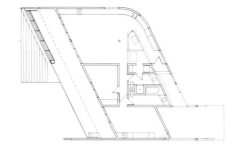

5 McDonald House, Stinson Beach,
California. 1987.

6 McDonald House. Plan and
elevation.

5

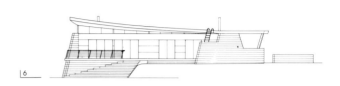

6

7

7 McDonald House. View of main
living space showing curved wall.

8

Stanley Saitowitz was born

in 1948 in Johannesburg, South

Africa. He is a graduate of

the University of Witwatersrand

Johannesburg, and the University

of California at Berkeley,

where he received his M. Arch.

He practices architecture in San

Francisco and teaches at Berkeley.

a driftwood crust protecting an iridescent interior charged with sunlight. . . . Remembering ships and boats, a prow protects the deck from the winds and alludes to the open sea."

Farther south, in Riverside, California, Saitowitz undertook his first public building, the conversion of an old department store into the California Museum of Photography. He describes the building as "a camera in which people are the film. . . . At the entry to the museum is the original camera, suspended over the front door, so that the beginning of the building is the beginning of photography. . . . The entry to the pinhole camera is via the balcony, so that one previews the view before the camera. . . . The ambience of the space is dark, with beams of light." The result—an inserted machine or pier structure—again displays a simplicity of approach, which augurs well for the future of Saitowitz as a designer of major buildings.

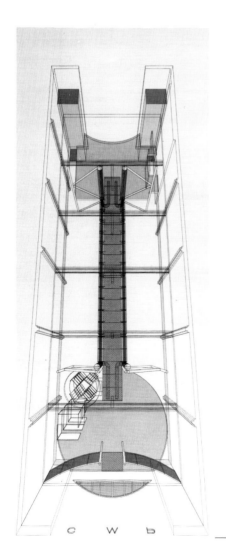

⌊8 *California Museum of Photography, Riverside, California. 1986. Model of new facade.*

__9⌋ *California Museum of Photography. Bird's-eye perspective showing camera elements of building.*

_1_|

H O L T   H I N S H A W   P F A U   J O N E S

Holt Hinshaw Pfau Jones are among a group of young American architects (along with Kaplan/Krueger and Neil Denari) whose work, as yet, has no collective label. It is at once technologically sophisticated and user-friendly, witty and satisfyingly intellectual. It is also highly sculptural, which is why the work is as likely to be found in galleries like the Storefront for Art and Architecture in New York as on the UCLA campus, where the firm is completing the Chiller and Cogeneration Plant, which provides chilled water and steam to technical laboratories.

The members of the practice believe, and have said publicly in lectures, that during the twentieth century the relationship between machines and architecture somehow went sour. Pointing out that machines are no better than their masters, the architects embrace the fallibility of scientific advance as a cause for celebration rather than an occasion for paranoia.

The summation of this concept is in their Astronauts Memorial, currently under construction at the Kennedy Space Center. This monument commemorates not only the astronauts killed in the *Challenger* space shuttle but also those who died earlier. The convention of inscribing the names of the dead on a polished granite tablet is observed; the huge tablet (42 by 50 feet) is lit by sunlight from reflected mirrors, and the whole memorial—slab, mirrors, and viewing platform—moves horizontally and vertically, tracking the sun by day, repositioning itself by night.

In the Right Away Redy Mix 1 and 2 cement factory and administration block in Oakland, California, machines inspired and articulated the buildings. With its exposed staircases, catwalks, ramps, and ducts, it deliberately recalls the midwestern grain silos of

_2_

⌞3⌟

⌞2___ *Right Away Redy Mix 2,*
Oakland, California. 1987. Elevation.

___3⌟ *Right Away Redy Mix 2. Elevation*
detail.

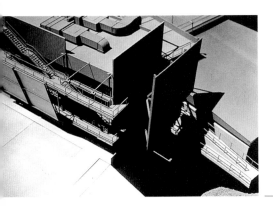

6

Paul Holt graduated from the

University of Manchester, England;

Marc Hinshaw, from the University

of California, Berkeley; Peter

Pfau, from Columbia University;

and Wes Jones, from the Harvard

Graduate School of Design.

Holt and Hinshaw set up shop

together in 1981, and in 1987 they

were joined by Pfau and Jones.

147

the '20s and '30s and imparts the same sense of confidence that was present in the days before technophobia paralyzed the public—one can see and understand what is going on.

"Redy Mix has some incredibly beautiful machines on the site," says Peter Pfau. "In fact, some parts of the building were intended to be manufactured by the same people who make those cement-mixing machines out of quarter-inch-plate steel. It's almost camouflaged. We put steel together in an incredibly straightforward way. It's not mitered, it's lap-jointed and spot-welded, and the joints aren't even ground smooth. You do it as directly and simply as you can, and that's the character of the thing." The kind of thing that looks as if it's been put together in a garage reflects, for them, "a uniquely American mechanical sensibility."

This is not to say that anyone can do it. The Altman & Manley office building, for an advertising agency in San Francisco, looks straight enough from the streetfront, but inside it uses architecture as an "organizing machine," a concept that few architects today can exploit. Spaces are not defined by walls, nor work stations simply by desks. The open-plan office can be subdivided for conferences, presentations, and exhibitions by walls of rolling overhead partitions that are based on the up-and-over garage-door mechanism. The underside of these rollers demarcates the public and the private sectors.

7

7 Altman & Manley Office, San Francisco. 1988. Interior, showing roller partitions.

Zvi Hecker's most recent project is The Spiral, an eight-story
apartment building on a gentle sloping site north of Tel Aviv,

ZVI HECKER fifty yards above the Mediterranean. It follows
the pattern of a spiral staircase, greatly magnified, with an
apartment on each step. By rotating each "step" floor by 22.5
degrees, open terraces are created at one end of each apartment and arcaded walkways at the other. The staircase "treads"
are edged with harsh gray metal, which projects jaggedly
through the soft white curves of the encircling walls. Hecker likes
startling contrasts: here the sophisticated concept of a building
spinning away from its tight central axis in a controlled series
of curves is nearly vitiated by the introduction of mock vernacular materials. But Hecker's choice of rough-cut stone topped
with stucco, which looks like snow over a Mediterranean patio,
has a long history, as does the idea of the spiral itself. "Its roots,"
he says, "reach back to Phoenician monolithic construction, the
Arab flat-roof terrace tradition, and the Middle Eastern courtyard
pattern. It is activated by the futurist rotational symmetry and
makes use of Russian Constructivist coherence, though disguised
and orientalized."

Hecker has been exploring helical and spiral forms in residential architecture since the early 1960s, organizing them around
a central courtyard, with a shifting formation of floors enveloped
in circular walls. Undoubtedly influenced by the architecture of
Samarkand, where he grew up, Hecker has developed one of
the earliest tower forms (seen first in the Cairo mosque of Ibn
Tulun) into something appropriate for today's desert dweller.

The same idea illuminates his plan for the City Center at Ramat
Hasharon (near Tel Aviv), a residential complex of 240 apartments. Still in the design stage, the project provides a cluster
of buildings, courtyards, and terraces that follow the geometric

⌐1   *The Spiral, Ramat Gan, Israel.*
1989. View from below.

⌐2   *The Spiral. Elevation.*

⌐2

Zvi Hecker was born in Krakow, Poland, in 1931 and spent his teenage years in Samarkand, U.S.S.R. He returned to Krakow for a year to study at the Polytechnic School of Architecture before emigrating to Israel in 1950. He continued his education at Technion Israel Institute of Technology, Haifa, and at the Avni Academy of Art, Tel Aviv, graduating in 1957. Military service for two years employed him in the Corps of Engineers, Israel Defense Forces. He set up private practice in 1959, working first with Eldar Sharon and then Alfred Neumann. He has taught as a visiting professor in Canada, the United States, and Europe.

3

3 The Spiral. Detail.

4 |

pattern of the sunflower. In this case, the spirals are spread out horizontally, radiating from the head of the flower in a series of arabesques.

The Jerusalem Synagogue, a 320-seat structure designed as part of a housing complex, brings together elements of the common Semitic heritage of Jews and Arabs. The steel triangle of the synagogue cuts through an enclosure of black, Kaaba-like stones. The interior of the building is illuminated by indirect light, which is introduced through the three towers in each corner; the contrast between the bright and dark areas of the ceiling creates a reflected image of the Star of David.

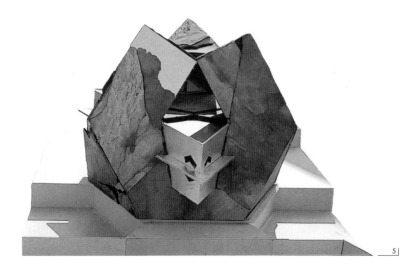

5 |

5 | _The Synagogue, Jerusalem. 1988. Model._

6 City Center, Ramat Hasharon,
Israel. 1989. Model.

7 City Center. Plan.

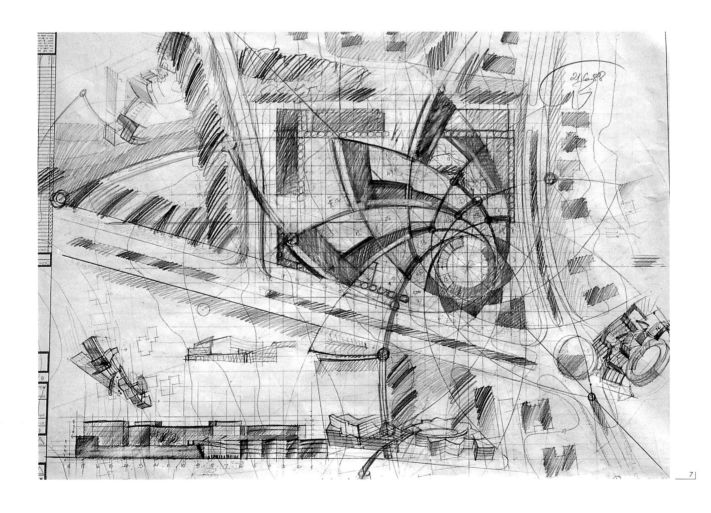

⌐1⌐

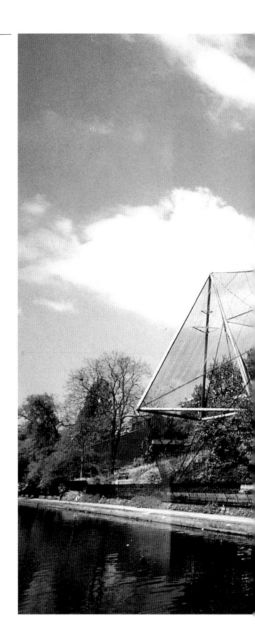

Even if the Fun Palace, commissioned by Joan Littlewood, had been built in 1961, it would not be standing today. A life span

C E D R I C   P R I C E of only ten years was envisioned by the architect, who felt it would become obsolete after a decade. It is one of the paradoxes of Cedric Price that he has chosen to work in a permanent medium with temporary structures, just as he chooses to be the best-dressed member of the Labour Party, a political group not known for its sartorial elegance.

But look beyond the famous starched collar, and what you will find throughout his work is a consistent commitment to movement: not just the horizontal movement of cranes rolling along the gantries, dropping prefabricated sections into place for a week or a month; not just the passage of people in and out of cities day and night, nor even of birds in the net of the Regent's Park aviary; but the linear movement of buildings through time, buildings that are born, that mature, age, decay, and die. Price hates corpses that should have been interred years ago. Because many of his own buildings are temporary structures, he has no interest in preserving structures that have outlived their usefulness.

He would as cheerfully demolish the Houses of Parliament to replace them with something more appropriate to the end of the twentieth century (helicopter pads, automated information-retrieval systems, etc.) as he would demolish a lodge so he could erect a gamekeeper's cottage (which he did). And the fact that the present owner has added three feet of Cotswold stone facing to the previously unadorned fireplace does not faze him at all. Price expects such things, for in the end he believes in the value of user participation. Students, politicians, artists, householders, even perhaps the birds should all be able to voice their needs to the architect, who will respond with a flexible building.

⌐2⌐

⌐2⌐ *Pop-up Parliament, London. 1965. View from enlarged Westminster Square.*

3 | Potteries Thinkbelt, Staffordshire,
England. 1964. View across the
transfer area at high level (left);
axonometric (right).

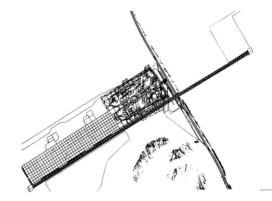

3

Cedric Price was born in 1934

in Stone, Staffordshire, England.

He was educated at Cambridge

and at the AA. He taught at

the AA from 1958 to 1964 and

founded his own practice in 1960.

With the engineer Frank Newby

he co-founded the Lightweight

Enclosures Unit, London, in

1969. Two years later he founded

Polyark Architectural Schools

Network. He is a member of the

Royal Institute of British Architects

and president of the Hot Stuff

Club.

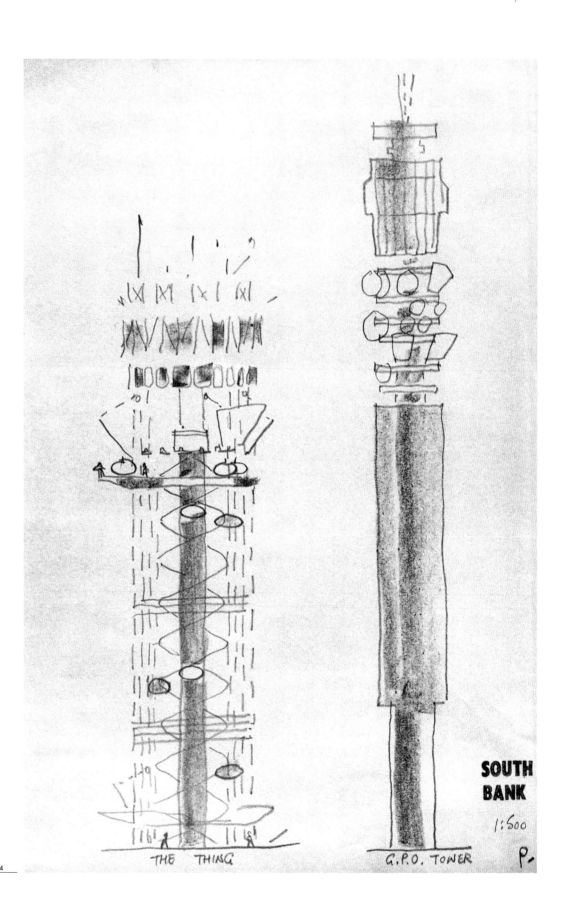

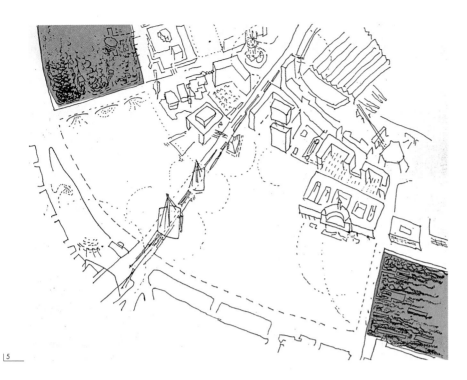

The fact that Price has been wrong about some predictions of the future does not negate the value of his ideas. Like most clever people, he sometimes assumes too much on the part of the users. In an ideal world, modular houses would be expanded or contracted as families changed. That most families obstinately prefer dolls' houses of brick, with sloping roofs and smoke curling out of the chimney, is not the architect's fault. If Price does not always inhabit the real world but a Bentham-inspired utopia, he does have the ability to look so far ahead that proposals may not catch up with him this time round. The idea of floating dams to contain oil spills—simple, radical, feasible—must be adopted before the end of the century. Other ideas may take a little longer.

___6| *South Bank. Top-deck plan of The Thing.*

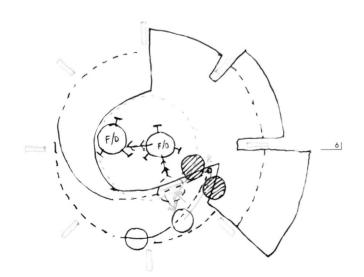

|6|

|7___ *South Bank. Model of The Thing.*

|7___

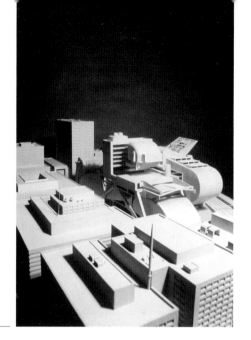

Of all the young American architects associated with the term "machine architecture," Neil Denari comes closest to creating a symbiotic language that clearly parallels characteristics of twentieth-century vehicles and appliances, whereby the "engine" and **N E I L   D E N A R I** the "casing" are given appropriate but interrelated form.

Denari's connection to the world of machines cannot be explained simply by the fact that he is the son of a helicopter engineer and has worked in the graphics department of a helicopter company himself. In his own words: "To make a Husserlian description of a collaboration between time and machines is obvious. The machine may be considered as in the world yet displaced in turn by its almost daily modification. This continuous, almost self-perpetuating regeneration speaks of the now of the machine, describing technology's development as inevitable as time itself."

A typical—and heroic—example of his work is the project called Adam's House in Paradise, in New York City. He describes it as a "slab-machine that is a hybrid of two housing types. The first floors are typical New York walk-up apartments, with stairs entered from the street. Above, riding on pilotis, is an external-corridor *Unité*-type slab. Affixed to the slab as mechanical appendages are cooperative functions such as the game room, laundry, and library. . . . The completed object is seen as a wall of observation witnessing nature's productivity." What Denari cannot say himself is that in this project (as in others) his exquisite eye is at work, weighing the formal balance of objects and determining just when to indulge in a curved surface or in an apparently distorted plane.

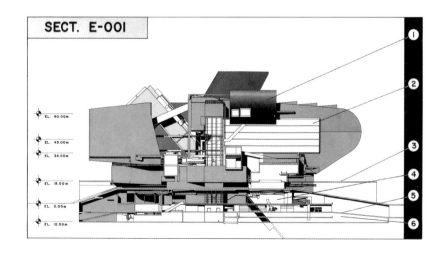

1___ *Tokyo International Forum, Tokyo. 1989. Model.*

2_| *Tokyo International Forum. Section.*

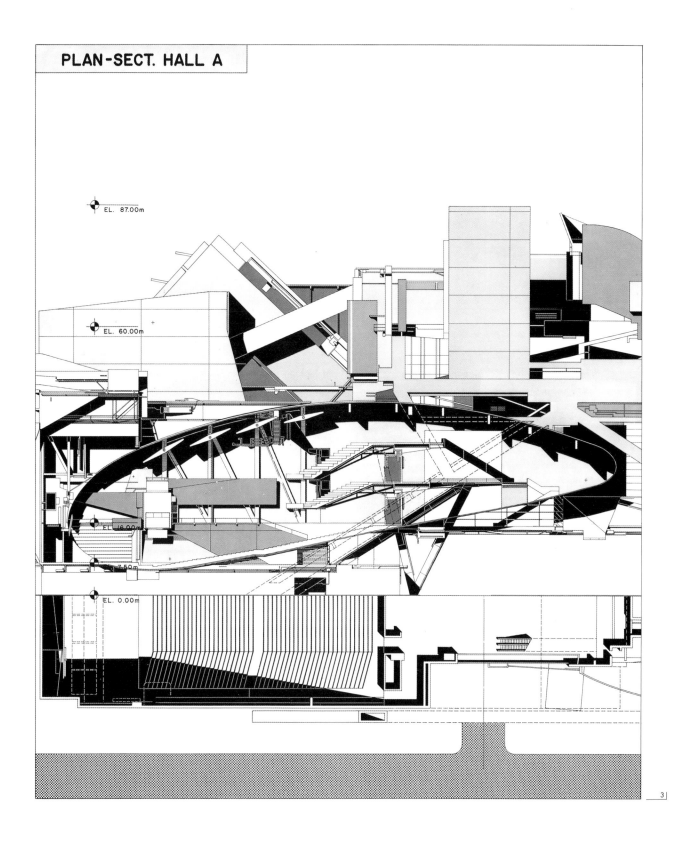

PLAN-SECT. HALL A

EL. 87.00m

EL. 60.00m

EL. 16.00m

EL. 7.50m

EL. 0.00m

Neil Denari was born in Fort

Worth, Texas, in 1957.

He received his B.Arch. in 1980

from the University of Houston

and his M.Arch. in 1982 from

Harvard, where he also studied the

philosophy of science. After work-

ing for Aerospatiale Hélicoptres

in Paris for several months, he

moved to New York, where he

taught at Columbia University.

In 1986 Denari established his

own firm, COR-TEX. He has lived

in Los Angeles since 1988, and he

currently teaches at SCI-ARC.

5

Denari's work has grown out of his understanding of Le Corbusier and the strict discussions at Harvard's Graduate School of Design in the early 1980s, along with a complementary set of enthusiasms fostered, perhaps, by the opportunities of the University of Houston's space-research building program. In the Solar Clock project of 1986, the unlikely skeleton around which the Denari machines creep is that of the Tower of London. More recently he has developed strong responses to Los Angeles, where he was a finalist in the West Coast Gateway competition, and Tokyo, where he was awarded third prize in the Tokyo International Forum competition, chosen over hundreds of corporate teams, whiz kids, and trained "urbanists."

Denari has great capacities as a teacher and a debator, and he is a listener, able to digest other people's outpourings in a state of quiet discrimination. Unlike many of his contemporaries, he is not one to lash out with a prejudicial one-liner; instead, half an hour later he will respond simply with a brilliant solution or observation.

In his work he combines a literary quality with a good-natured enthusiasm for technology and a sound architectural understanding. This suggests that his built work, when it comes, will have consequence, and will probably continue to develop long after the "machine architecture" conversation has ceased to amuse.

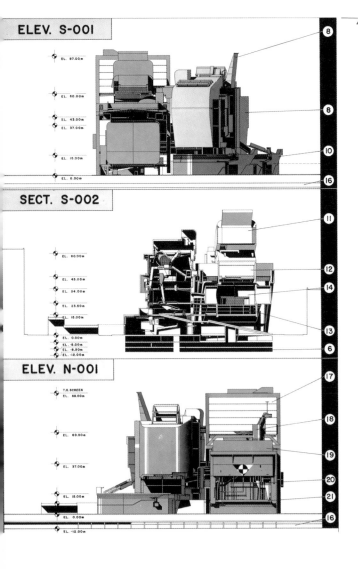

4 | Tokyo International Forum.
South elevation, section, and north elevation.

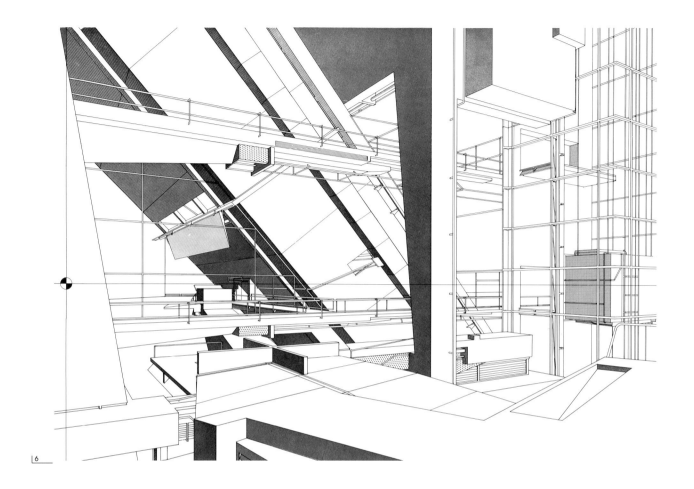

└6

└6___ *Tokyo International Forum.*
Perspective view between Hall A and
multipurpose gallery.

└7___ *Tokyo International Forum.*
Model.

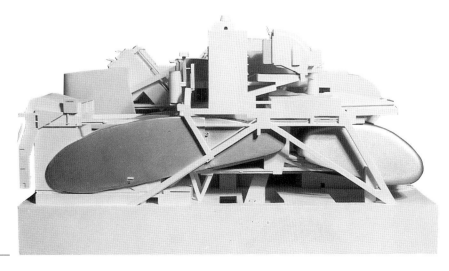

└7

R O N H E R R O N

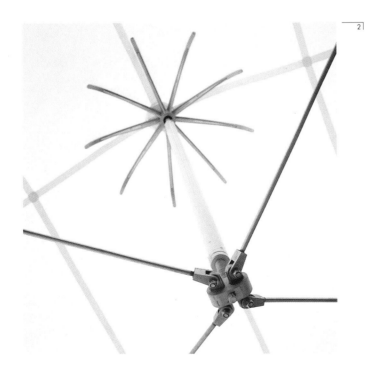

"The return of Ron" was the theme of the British architectural press in 1989, when his conversion of two Edwardian buildings in London's West End was unveiled. But he has never really been away. It is impossible to imagine the English architectural scene over the last twenty-five years without seeing his familiar bearded figure, invariably clad in jeans, solid, friendly, reassuring, and—above all—there. In fact, everything about Herron the man is the antithesis of his work. From the H.G. Wells nightmare of his Walking City (1964), done with the Archigram group, through the inflatable dome for the Bubble Theater Company in London (1978), to his latest conversion for Imagination, a design-based company, the idea of illusion, reality, instability, and pure fantasy has emerged as a continuing theme.

It was no surprise to his friends when Herron became one of the first architects to realize the possibilities of computer-aided design (CAD) as the rest of us were still climbing out of the 1970s. For what is more unreal than walking through a building that exists only on the screen? Of course, CAD is another tool on the designer's table, but few architects have exploited it and reveled in it as fully as Herron. A strong impetus came from his two sons, Andrew and Simon, both architects and computer buffs, who made up the rest of Herron Associates (now merged with Imagination). But even prior to their involvement, Herron was moving into the creation of "see-through" architecture, as in his designs for the DOM Office Headquarters in Cologne, Germany (with Cook & Hawley), and the Wonderworld Theme Park at Corby, Northamptonshire, England.

He continued to work with members of Archigram after the group split up, and his last joint project was an unrealized scheme for La Défense, Paris, a competition project with the late Warren

3|

4| *Imagination Headquarters. Section through atrium.*

5| *Imagination Headquarters. Front facade at night.*

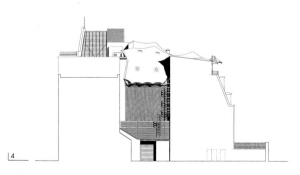

4|

5|

*Ron Herron was born in London
in 1930. He worked with the now
defunct Greater London Council
from 1954 to 1961 on public
schemes, then became a founding
member of the Archigram group
and co-editor of its magazine.
He practiced with several London
firms before setting up his own
company in 1982 with his two
sons, Andrew and Simon. He has
taught as a unit master at the
AA since 1965 and has acted as a
visiting lecturer at numerous universities in Europe and America.*

Chalk. Although the seeds of Herron's recent work are present in his early projects—his style has never undergone a radical shift—there has been a gradual stripping away, so that today it has become refined to the point of minimalism. For Herron the celebration of the space between the struts is as important as the struts themselves.

Herron may be a dreamer, a fantasist, but there is usually pragmatic reasoning behind his proposals. For their headquarters the Imagination Company wanted to amalgamate two buildings of unequal height into one. The architect's solution was to throw a lightweight opaque structure across the gap, bridging it with a delicate net that provides an airy, toplit space, crossed by a series of walkways. He overcame the objections of planning and fire-department authorities to create an extraordinary yet practical annex that has rightly won praise, both from those who have just "discovered" Herron and from those who knew he was there all along.

8 Imagination Headquarters. Rear roof gallery.

Bernard Tschumi's career and reputation as a teacher-analyst
serve as encouragement to those who believe that architecture

B E R N A R D   T S C H U M I should develop through a
series of intellectual processes. Yet, at the same time, it is clear
that he is more than just an abstractionist.

His early work is best summarized by the series of drawings
that were published in 1981 as *The Manhattan Transcripts*, a
kind of cross-fertilization between dramatic event, body movement, figuration, and architectural pattern. This project exposed
the particular power of Tschumi's creativity: his ability to analyze
the motivating forces of a design, to articulate them as "types"
or "actions" or "forms," and then to reassemble them in a very
clear architectural hierarchy. He has created a special diagrammatic language or system that is instantly recognizable (though
the parts are not repeated from scheme to scheme), and it has
been used to inform the Parc de la Villette, the New National
Theater in Tokyo, the Strasbourg County Hall, Ponts-Villes in
Lausanne, and the Karlsruhe media center, among other projects.

It was probably this clarity of thought and a seeming inevitability
of the parts, along with an identifiable "game," that won him
the La Villette competition. In the years since then, he has used
the opportunity of building the various follies to move onward,
out of an emblematic or quasi-quotational phase and into a
new mode of invention. This new style owes much to the more
technical architecture made possible by the Centre Beaubourg
by Piano and Rogers, but it has an almost space-age élan that
often escapes the English so-called high-tech architects. This
is most clearly demonstrated in his plans for the Kansai Airport,
where a wild series of core components zigzag across the space
between the waiting areas, which are held by an equally eccentric series of pylons.

1　New Kansai International
Airport, Osaka, Japan. 1988.
Structure.

2　Kansai Airport. Aerial view.

3　Kansai Airport. Section model.

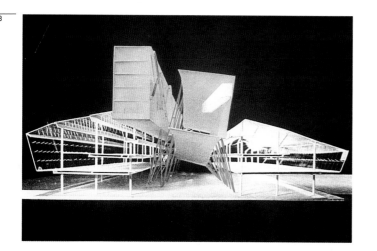

4] ZKM Center for Art and Media
Technology, Karlsruhe, Germany.
1989. Interior walkways.

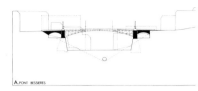

A. PONT BESSIERES

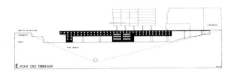

E. PONT DES TERREAUX

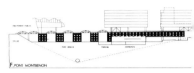

F. PONT MONTBENON

In his architecture, elements are often "cast" across space; the linear systems help to clearly maintain the identity of the principal zone. We see this in the Ponts-Villes for Lausanne, where five Tschumi bridges carry on the dynamic suggested by two existing bridges in the city. In the Tokyo theater the demarcation of zones and carrying strands was reminiscent of the musical stave. The clarity and wit of the scheme was exemplary, and though it may have been too cool for a Japanese audience, it remains an object lesson for students of architectural planning.

By the time of the ZKM project, a competition for a new media center in Karlsruhe, Tschumi was able to thrust pieces of "wild" architecture between pieces of "hard" architecture in a manner that went far beyond the studiousness of the La Villette pavilions. Even in the earlier work, though, the ease and directness of the objects were proof of Tschumi's architectural maturity, especially given the layers of reference and meaning that inform them.

5| ZKM. South elevation.

6| ZKM. Floor plans for second level.

7| Ponts-Villes, Lausanne, Switzerland 1988. Sections through the bridges.

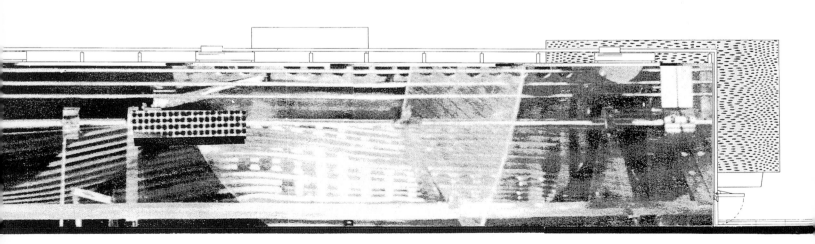

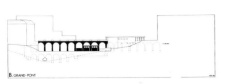

B. GRAND-PONT

C. METROPONT

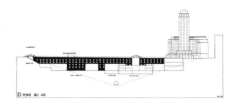

D. PONT BEL-AIR

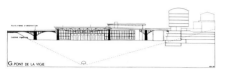

G. PONT DE LA VIGIE

H. PONT CHAUDERON

7

6

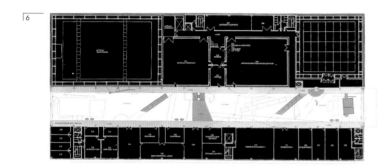

Bernard Tschumi was born in 1944 of French/Swiss parentage. He studied at the Federal Institute of Technology in Zurich, where he received his degree in architecture in 1969. He taught at the AA, London, for ten years, and at the Institute for Architecture and Urban Studies, Princeton University, and Cooper Union. After winning the international competition for the Parc de la Villette in Paris in 1983, he formed Bernard Tschumi Architects, with offices in New York and Paris. He is a Chevalier des Arts et des Lettres and a Chevalier of the Legion of Honor. He is presently dean of Columbia University's Graduate School of Architecture, Planning, and Preservation.

5

1 Shonandai Cultural Center,
Kanagawa, Japan. 1989.
Main entrance showing ramp
into Tasmania.

ITSUKO HASEGAWA

2 Shonandai Cultural Center.
Side elevation.

Itsuko Hasegawa had designed some twenty buildings before
the completion in 1989 of the extraordinary and exuberant
Shonandai Cultural Center.
Many of them are known for their simplicity and their lack of
rhetoric. Indeed, it seemed for some years as if Hasegawa fit
very neatly into the role of the first prominent woman architect
in Japan by designing a series of houses that were concerned
with the domestic program more than anything else. "I once went
on a trip . . . to look at folk houses in northern Japan," she says,
"and on that trip I came to understand what Shinohara had
meant when he said that folk houses should be seen not from the
outside but from the inside. Ever since, I've gone to look at folk
houses and old cityscapes, drawn by a desire not to develop
a new architectural concept of tradition but to learn how architecture might be made into something people can immediately
relate to. It wasn't that I wanted to analyze their forms or details.
I wanted to confirm the presence . . . of something more fundamental than architecture."

Yet despite such modesty, Hasegawa has displayed over the
years an ever-expanding "eye." The early houses are mainly for
young couples with limited resources, and out of such restraint
Hasegawa developed a determined system. "In House 2 in
Yaizu, I thought of the building as an accumulation of fragments.
The house was also the first building in which there was a clear
separation between the structural frame and the outer membrane.
This approach was developed further in the stationery store in
Yaizu, and I have continued to use it. . . . In House 2 I discovered how to create a rational structural order and then to wrap
around it membranes with different expressive qualities, some
that can be interpreted only as irrational."

Itsuko Hasegawa was born in 1941 in Shizuoka Prefecture, Japan, and graduated from the School of Architecture at Kantogakuin University in 1963. She worked in the office of Kiyonori Kikutake for five years before studying with Kazuo Shinohara at the Tokyo Institute of Technology. From 1971 to 1976 she worked with Shinohara, and then established her own practice. She has received several annual awards from the Architectural Institute of Japan and the Japan Inter-Design Conference.

3| *Atelier in Tomigaya, Tokyo. 1986. Front elevation.*

4 House in Kuwabara, Matsuyama,
Ehime, Japan. 1980. Front elevation.

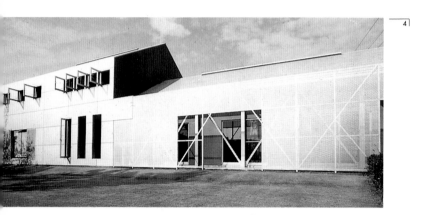

4

By 1980, in a house in Kuwabara, Matsuyama, Hasegawa had created an apparently rational diagram, so that envelope, framework, and room arrangement could be developed as required, and a "layered" series of spaces resulted. Such a method is extended in the N.C. House in Nakano, Tokyo, where it is applied to a necessarily more cellular structure (a block of apartments). "In this chaotic corner of town, which sharply contrasts with nearby skyscrapers, I wanted to build a clear, transparent, and fresh-looking building," says Hasegawa. Much of the freshness comes from her ability to peel away entire elements of the architecture from the defining diagram and its primary framework. In the mid-1980s she began to deal with institutional buildings, such as Bizan Hall (a college building), and develop her characteristic tailored roof lights and layers of perforated-metal filters, which provide an almost Gothic quality of light and diffusion of space toward the interiors. Borrowed high-tech devices are also found in this building, but by the end of the 1980s these are jettisoned in favor of a more sequential language of parts.

Both the pavilion for Artec '89 in Nagoya and the Shonandai Cultural Center create virtual landscapes of objects, which take the form of trees, hills, or pavilions and, when necessary, are quite heroic—as in the case of the three domes that top off the Shonandai composition. Resolving the large-scale program, which calls for an auditorium, social rooms, a gymnasium, and a children's center, among other elements, is dependent on providing a sense of place in this particularly characterless extremity of the Tokyo conurbation. Hasegawa's sophisticated control of sequential space, the use of "hot" and then "cool" articulation, the clarity of circulation, and the simplicity of detail are the unexpected characteristics of the building itself; these qualities are very telling in

5

5   Bizan Hall, Shizuoka, Japan.
1984. Interior.

a culture which is highly male chauvinist and allows
the generation of Hasegawa, Toyo Ito, and Kazunari
Sakamoto only a peripheral role.

Interestingly enough, the experience of the building
recalls that of James Stirling's Staatsgalerie in Stuttgart
in several ways: the rhetorical hillside presented
to the town center, the path through as opposed to
the path within, the notability of many of the internal
spaces, and the wit of the high iconography used at
key points. "I'm often accused by other architects of
being too optimistic," Hasegawa says. "They say that
my buildings are not critical of society or combative. I
have great doubts that a building ought to be combative toward society." This statement seems to embody
the present direction of her work.

⌞6___ *House in Nerima; Tokyo. 1986.*
Moon-viewing pavilion.

‾7⌝ *House in Nerima. Interior stairs.*

‾7⌝

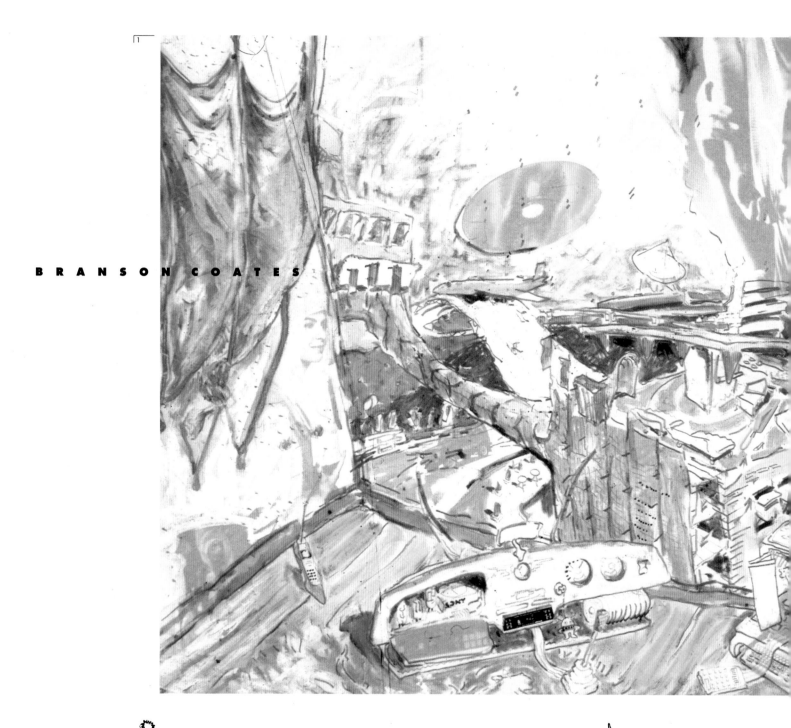

B R A N S O N   C O A T E S

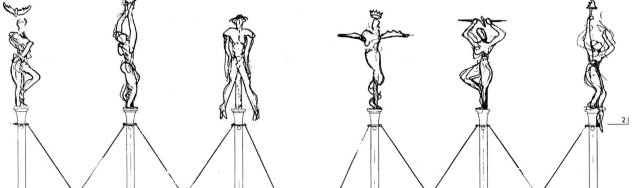

In 1984 Nigel Coates had designed only two interiors—his own London apartment and that of a friend, Jasper Conran. Today he is the best-known English architect in Japan and the British media are nominating him as the "architectural voice" of the 1990s. It is ironic that the Japanese gave him the chance to realize his anarchic/classical themes. As Coates and his partner, Doug Branson, point out, if their ideas seem strange in London, with its broad-based tolerance of the bizarre, how much stranger they must seem in conventional Japan.

Their first project there, the Metropole, which draws on English gentlemen's clubs and elements of eighteenth-century Gothic, was theatrical, authentic, romantic, and elitist. English artists were commissioned to provide specific items—chandeliers by Tom Dixon, painted pelmets by Zaza Wentworth Stanley, brass castings by Valerie Robertson—and in this way the finished interior became a showcase for the explosion of talent in 1980s London. The Metropole was followed quickly by the Caffè Bongo, with its crashed-airplane interiors, and the Takeo Kikuchi Bohemia Club.

During this period, Coates was pursuing a different theme through his teaching at the AA and the formation of the NATO group (Narrative Architecture Today). NATO delighted in exploiting punk street culture, recycling objects, proposing wild, anarchic schemes for huge areas of London, and building models from junk. Drawings became larger and were splashed onto walls, canvases, cardboard—anything that came to hand. No matter how chaotic their work looked to the viewer, they always maintained control.

In 1988 Branson Coates completed their first building in Japan, the Noah's Ark restaurant and bar in Sapporo. On a narrow,

2| *Nishi Azabu Wall, Tokyo. 1989. Detail drawing for facade screen.*

3| *Nishi Azabu Wall. Drawing by Nigel Coates.*

Doug Branson was born in 1951
and studied at the Canterbury
School of Art and Architecture
and the AA in London. He taught
at the AA from 1975 to 1977
and at Canterbury in 1976.
He has worked in England for
the Department of Education and
Science and for private practices
in London and New York.

4 Noah's Ark, Sapporo, Japan.
1987. Exterior.

5 Noah's Ark. Interior.

6 Noah's Ark. East elevation.

triangular site overlooking the river, they created an extraordinary object, which thrusts forward with the great prow of the ark but slides into regular classical (this time Etruscan) facades on the upper floor. Windows on the river side lean out like projections from a wooden sailing ship. Construction methods and costs alone would have made this building remarkable—the cost of the prow, formed from concrete sprayed on nets, doubled the original budget. In addition, though, the scheme demonstrates a skillful use of imagery and sophisticated spatial handling. The ground-floor bar uses nonstructural columns to form a sectional sequence of friendly spaces, while the curved beams that cross the central stem of the ark tie it to the restaurant above.

The idea for the Nishi Azabu Wall in Tokyo, a constructed piece of "Roman" wall infilled with "industrial jetsam of the twentieth century," was a response to the request for a building "that would last forever." Preliminary drawings show a structure that is evocative to Western eyes, exploding behind its mock antique front into something rich and bizarre—one of England's most successful exports to Japan.

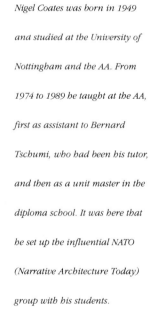

Nigel Coates was born in 1949 and studied at the University of Nottingham and the AA. From 1974 to 1989 he taught at the AA, first as assistant to Bernard Tschumi, who had been his tutor, and then as a unit master in the diploma school. It was here that he set up the influential NATO (Narrative Architecture Today) group with his students.

Branson Coates Architecture was established in 1985.

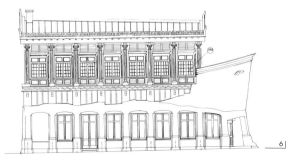

6

1| *Ersting Factory, Coesfeld-Lette,
Germany. 1985. Facade.*

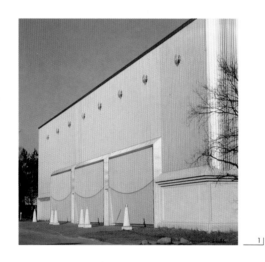

___1|

S A N T I A G O   C A L A T R A V A

2| *Bach de Roda—Felipe II Bridge,
Barcelona. 1987.*

3 | *Wohlen High School, Aargau, Switzerland. 1988. Auditorium.*

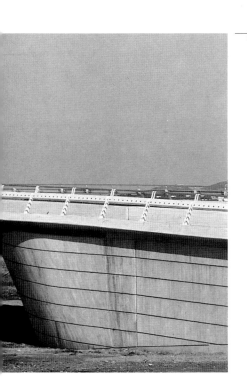

2

The Auguste Perret Prize for applied technology in architecture was particularly appropriate in the case of Santiago Calatrava, who won the award in 1987. He has rekindled the essential quality of the earlier designer's work: the central role played by the integrity of primary structure in defining original form. Calatrava's work cuts through the laziness evident in buildings that fail to pursue potential geometries, a laziness that has been tolerated since the time of Nervi.

A subconscious recognition of this quality may well have contributed to the enormous enthusiasm for Calatrava's work among today's very young architects. His road bridge in Barcelona, which links Felipe II and Bach de Roda, has become an icon not only of structural daring but of aesthetic cheekiness: the splitting of the arched bands becomes a structural and an artistic release as the entire bridge fans out in plan.

Calatrava is an engineer and an architect, and he seems to identify with both disciplines. In the factory at Coesfeld—designed jointly with Bruno Reichlin and Fabio Reinhardt—his personal contribution was the creation of eccentric surfaces and spaces, particularly in the canopies and the bridge-link. This is a fascinating collaboration because his colleagues have a considerable reputation as hard-edged, even rather rationalist, architects. Similarly, in the Stadelhofen Station, the brilliance of the structural components in the fishbonelike scheme is offset by the nonchalance with which the curve of the track and the adjacent hillside are accommodated. The four typologies of structure and envelope at the Wohlen High School are virtuoso essays in technique and pure architectural form.

Suhr Concert Hall, Bärenmatte
suhr Aargau, Switzerland. 1988.
Detail of auditorium structure.

Santiago Calatrava was born in Valencia, Spain, in 1951 and obtained his degree from the Institute of Architecture there. In 1979 he received an engineering degree from the Federal Institute of Technology in Zurich, and two years later received his doctorate in technical sciences. The same year, he opened an architecture and engineering office in Zurich. Most of his realized work has been in Switzerland and Spain, where he has exhibited his designs and won several awards. In 1987 he won the Auguste Perret Prize for applied technology in architecture.

Despite his explosive presence on the European scene (he is building in Switzerland, Germany, Spain, and England) and his quick progress to an almost guru-like status, his commissions usually fall short of *total* building enclosures. If we look, for instance, at the roof of the concert hall at Suhr and then extrapolate an image of an entire building, we can sense the real challenge that his designs might offer to the general thrust of architecture. Calatrava's work has both style and inevitability; it is aware of scale and "fit" but relies only on itself; it has no need for applied stylization; it does not imitate.

6

6   *Extension of Stadelhofen Railway Station, Zurich. 1988.*

P R O J E C T   L I S T S

A K S   R U N O

Competition entry for Olympic West, Los Angeles, 1988 (finalist)

Metapolis: Los Angeles, 1988 (project)

Competition entry for Alexandria Library, Alexandria, Egypt, 1989 (first special mention)

Competition entry for Tokyo International Forum, Tokyo, 1989

La Place Jacques-Cartier, Montreal, 1990 (project)

ALSOP AND LYALL

Proposal for Riverside Studios, London, 1981

Sundance Studios (dance and health studios),
Hammersmith, London, 1981

Building for a Media Center, Cologne, Germany, 1987

Sheringham Leisure Pool, Norfolk, England, 1988

Renovation of Tottenham Hale Station, Tottenham, London, 1989

Canary Wharf Control Tower and Lifting Bridge,
Docklands, London, 1989

Hafenstrasse Workshops and Apartments, Hamburg, Germany, 1989

Tower Project, Herouville St. Clair, France, 1989

British Pavilion, Expo '92, Seville, Spain, 1989 (project)

Thamesmead Town, London, 1989

River Project on the Garonne, Bordeaux, France, 1989

Family Hotel South Dock, Docklands, London, 1989

Renovation of the Corn Exchange, Leeds, England, 1990

Ferry Terminal, Hamburg, Germany, under construction 1990

ASYMPTOTE

Palmanova Memory Theater, Venice Biennale, 1985
(with Daniel Libeskind and Cranbrook Studio; thesis project of Hani
Rashid)

Sogli e Passaggi, installation for Milan Triennale, 1986
(with Daniel Libeskind)

Kursaal for an Evacuee, theoretical project, Artists Space Gallery,
New York, 1987

Concorso di Lanciano, competition entry for planning strategy and
building design, Lanciano, Italy, 1987

Steel Cloud, West Coast Gateway, Los Angeles, 1988–91

Competition entry for Alexandria Library, Alexandria, Egypt, 1989
(honorable mention)

Twenty-first-Century Paris (three projects for the Île de la Cité),
"Paris: Architecture and Utopia" exhibition, Pavillon de l'Arsenal, Paris,
1989–90

Optigraphs 1+2, constructions, Galerie Aedes, Berlin, 1990

BRANSON COATES

Gamma Tokyo, 1985 (project)

Conran House, London, 1985

Metropole Restaurant, Tokyo, 1985

Caffè Bongo, Tokyo, 1986

Takeo Kikuchi Barber Shop and Bohemia Jazz Club, Tokyo, 1986

Silver Jewelry Shop, London, 1987

Noah's Ark Restaurant, Sapporo, Japan, 1987

Jasper Conran Shop, Dublin, Republic of Ireland, 1987

Kings Cross Eurofields, London, 1988 (project)

Jigsaw Shop, Kensington, London, 1988

Katharine Hamnett Shop, Glasgow, Scotland, 1988

Stonehenge Shop, Salisbury, England, 1989

Hotel Otaru Marittimo, Otaru, Japan, 1989

Nishi Azabu Wall (commercial building), Tokyo, 1989

SANTIAGO CALATRAVA

Bridge at Disentis, Switzerland, 1979 (project)

Zupa Exposition Hall, Zurich, 1981 (with Martin Spühler)

Competition entry for Schwarzhaupt AG Building,
Dielsdorf, Germany, 1982 (first prize)

Competition entry for Rhine Bridge, Diepoldsau, Germany, 1982
(second prize; with Weser and Wolfensberger)

Portico and roof for Swiss Federal Railway reception hall,
Lucerne, Switzerland, 1984

Facade for Ersting Factory, Coesfeld-Lette, Germany, 1985
(with Reichlin and Reinhardt)

Bach de Roda–Felipe II Bridge, Barcelona, 1987

Remodeling of Tabourettli Cabaret Theater, Basel, Switzerland, 1987

Extension of Stadelhofen Railway Station, Zurich, 1988

Competition entry for Television Tower, Barcelona, 1988

Suhr Concert Hall, Bärenmatte suhr Aargau, Switzerland, 1988

Wohlen High School, Aargau, Switzerland, 1988

COOP HIMMELBLAU

Villa Rosa (prototype for a pneumatic living unit), 1968

Restless Sphere, Basel, Switzerland, 1971

House with Flying Roof, London, 1973

Large Cloud Scene, Vienna, 1976

Reiss Bar, Vienna, 1977

Blazing Wing, Graz, Austria, 1980

Red Angel Bar, Vienna, 1980–81

Open House, Malibu, California, 1983/89

Rooftop Remodeling, Vienna, 1984–89

Baumann Studio, Vienna, 1984

Skyline Project, Hamburg, Germany, 1985

Boutique Konyo Shente, Tokyo, 1986

Urban plan for the new town of Melun-Sénart, France, 1987

Restructuring of Ronacher Theater, Vienna, 1987

Funder Factory 3, St. Veit/Glan, Austria, 1988–89

NEIL DENARI

Adam's House in Paradise, New York, 1984

Heuristic Structure, 1984

Communications Center, Forth Worth, Texas, 1984

Monastery, New York, 1985

Solar Clock, London, 1986

Competition entry for City Hall, Leesburg, Virginia, 1987

Competition entry for Astronauts Memorial, Kennedy Space Center, Florida, 1987

Competition entry for West Coast Gateway, Los Angeles, 1988

Competition entry for Tokyo International Forum, Tokyo, 1989 (third prize)

Pool Regenerators, Los Angeles, 1989

GÜNTHER DOMENIG

Parish Center, Oberwart, Austria, 1969 (with Eilfried Huth)

Olympic Swimming Pool Pavilion, Munich, 1972 (with Huth)

Restaurant Nord, Olympic Stadium, Munich, 1972 (with Huth)

Teaching Academy, Graz Eggenberg, Austria, 1973 (with Huth)

Multipurpose Convent Hall, Graz Eggenberg, 1977

Z-Bank, Favoriten, Vienna, 1979

Dockyard, Wörthersee, Austria, 1981

Steindorf Bridge, Ossiachersee, Austria, 1982

Renovation of Rikki Reiner Boutique, Klagenfurt, Austria, 1984

Hotel and Congress Center, Salzburg, Austria, 1987

Stonehouse, Steindorf, Austria, 1989

Reconstruction of Z-Bank, Zollamtstrasse, Vienna, under construction 1990

Extension to Technical University, Graz, Austria, under construction 1990

EISELE + FRITZ

Trischler House, Nieder-Beerbach, 1982

German Library, Frankfurt, 1982 (project)

Competition entry for Post Museum, Frankfurt, 1982 (third prize)

Beckman House, Neu-Isenburg, 1983

Mehr House, Darmstadt, 1984

Hairdressing Salon, Darmstadt, 1984

Kaiser's Café, Darmstadt, 1985

Schrumpf House, Darmstadt, 1986

Seifert-Rothe House, Frankisch-Crumbach, 1986

Competition entry for Post Office, Hamburg, 1986 (first prize)

Bell-Broszeit House, Ober-Ramstadt, 1987

Weber House, Frankfurt Sossenheim, 1987

Station Entrance, Mainz, 1988 (project)

Children's and Cultural Center, Darmstadt-Eberstadt, 1988

Saalgasse House, Frankfurt, 1988

Town Hall Square, Darmstadt-Eberstadt, 1990

ALL LOCATIONS ARE IN GERMANY

FORMALHAUT

Cow Project, Vogelsberg, Germany, 1985

Rendezvous, Morfelden, Germany, 1985

House Extension for a Veterinarian, Gelnhausen, Germany, 1985

Installation, Gallery for Art and Architecture,
Hamburg, Germany, 1986

Installation, Galerie ROM, Oslo, Norway, 1987

Caravan, installation, Galerie Haffner, Munich, 1987

Houses for Singles, 1988

Anthropological Museum, Frankfurt, 1989 (project)

Double Knight Game, Frankfurt, 1989

Grand Prix, installation, Center for Contemporary National Art,
Grenoble, Spain, 1989

Full House, project for the Cultural Department,
Lilienstrasse, Germany, 1989

FRANK GEHRY

Addition to Ron Davies Studio, Malibu, California, 1977

Gehry House, Santa Monica, California, 1979

Cabrillo Marine Museum, San Pedro, California, 1979

House for a Filmmaker, Santa Monica Canyon, California, 1980

Law School Building, Loyola University, Los Angeles, 1981

Aerospace Museum, Los Angeles, 1982

Frances Howard Goldwyn Regional Branch Library, Hollywood,
California, 1983

The Temporary Contemporary, Museum of Contemporary Art,
Los Angeles, 1983

Borman House, Malibu, California, 1984

Norton House, Venice, California, 1984

Fishdance Restaurant, Kobe, Japan, 1986

Disney Concert Hall, Los Angeles, 1986

Kings Cross Development, London, 1989

Vitra International Furniture Manufacturing Facility and Design Museum,
Weil am Rhein, Germany, 1989

VOLKER GIENCKE

Dockyard, Wörthersee, Austria, 1981

Primary School, Graz, Austria, 1984

Maxonus Shop, Graz, 1985

Rosenhain Café-Restaurant, Graz, 1986

Benedek House, Graz, 1986

Headquarters for Porsche-Austria, Salzburg, Austria, 1987

Competition entry for West Coast Gateway, Los Angeles, 1988

House in the Mountains, Graz, 1988

Social Housing, Graz, 1988

Exhibition Hall and Teaching Facilities for Carpentry,
Styria, Austria, 1988

Reischl House, Graz, 1988

Rückenstuhl House, Graz, 1988

University Building, Graz, 1989

Judo Hall, Graz, under construction 1990

Botanical Gardens, Graz, under construction 1990

ZAHA HADID

Apartment Conversion, 59 Eaton Place, London, 1982

Competition entry for The Peak, Hong Kong, 1983 (first prize)

Competition entry for Grand Buildings, Trafalgar Square, London, 1985

Competition entry for Kurfürstendamm Office Building,
Berlin, 1986 (first prize)

Competition entry for West Hollywood Civic Center, Hollywood,
California, 1987

Competition entry for Al Wahda Sports Stadium, Abu Dhabi,
United Arab Emirates, 1988

Hafenstrasse Housing Project, Hamburg, Germany, 1989

Music-Video Pavilion, Groningen, Netherlands, 1990

Moonsoon Restaurant, Sapporo, Japan, 1990

Folly, Expo '90, Osaka, Japan, 1990

Tomigaya Building, Tokyo, under construction 1990

Vitra Fire Station, Weil am Rhein, Germany, under construction 1990

Media Park, Düsseldorf, Germany, under construction 1990

Azabu-Jyuban Building, Tokyo, under construction 1990

Glunz Wood Exhibition Pavilion, Cologne, Germany, under construction
1990

JASPER HALFMANN

Manhattan Transfer, permanent installation at P. S. 1,
Long Island City, New York, 1981

Competition entry for Prince Albrecht Palace, Berlin, 1984
(with Rebecca Horn and Klaus Zillich)

Cosmological Park (Calendar Square, Café Orangerie, and Rhizomatic
Bridge), Berlin, 1984–85 (with Zillich and Zilling)

Competition entry for Film Center Esplanade, Berlin, 1985
(first prize; with Zillich)

Competition entry for Platz der Republik, Berlin, 1986
(with FPB and Zillich)

Competition entry for Spree Bridge, Berlin, 1987 (first prize)

"Simultaneous Concepts," conceptual exhibition shown in Paris,
London, New York, Los Angeles, Tokyo, and Berlin, 1988

Architectural Eros Matrix, 1989

ITSUKO HASEGAWA

House 1 in Yaizu, Shizuoka, 1972

House in Midorigaoka, Tokyo, 1975

House 2 in Yaizu, 1977

Stationery Shop, Yaizu, 1978

Tokumara Children's Clinic, Ehime, 1979

House in Kuwabara, Matsuyama, Ehime, 1980

Aono Building, Ehime, 1982

House in Kanazawabunko, Kanagawa, 1983

N.C. House, Nakano, Tokyo, 1984

Bizan Hall, Shizuoka, 1984

House in Kumamoto, 1986

Atelier in Tomigaya, Tokyo, 1986

Sugai Internal Clinic, Ehime, 1986

House in Igashi-Tamagawa, Tokyo, 1986

House in Nerima, Tokyo, 1986

K.K. House, Tokyo, 1987

Shonandai Cultural Center, Kanagawa, 1989

Pavilion for Artec '89, Nagoya, 1989

ALL LOCATIONS ARE IN JAPAN

HAUS-RUCKER-CO.

Geteiltes Haus, Berlin, 1980

Art Museum and Federal Art Gallery, Bonn, 1984

Exhibition Hall for the Bonn Art Society
(conversion and extension of the Flowerhall), Bonn, 1984–86

Plaza (with U-bahn station and open-air theater),
Marienhof, Munich, 1985 (project)

Neuss Tower, Neuss, 1985

Kantdreieck Tower, Berlin, 1985

Museum Island, Hamburg, 1986 (project)

Lineares Haus (Linear House), Darmstadt, 1986

Treppenhaus (Step House), Berlin, 1986

Pfalztheater, Kaiserslautern, 1987 (project; with Thomas Gutt)

Hotel, Victoriagelande, Berlin, 1987 (project)

Media Park, Cologne, 1987 (project)

German Historical Museum, Berlin, 1988 (project)

House for Rauchstrasse, Berlin, 1988 (project)

Competition entry for ZKM Center for Art and Media Technology,
Karlsruhe, 1989

Entrance to the Radiation Protection and Environmental Research
Building, the Ring, Munich, 1989 (project)

ZVI HECKER

Synagogue, Military Academy, Negev Desert, Israel, 1969

City Center, Montreal, 1970

Synagogue, Ben-Gurion Airport, Tel Aviv, Israel, 1972

Monument, Negev Desert, 1975

Band Shell, Hatikva Park, Tel Aviv, 1978

Competition entry for Pahlavi National Library, Teheran, Iran, 1978

Ramot Housing, Jerusalem, 1982

Dormitories, Military Academy, Negev Desert, 1983

Serpent Art Museum, Palm Springs, California, 1986

The Synagogue, Jerusalem, 1988

City Center, Ramat Hasharon, Israel, 1989

Competition entry for Tokyo International Forum, Tokyo, 1989

The Spiral, Ramat Gan, Israel, 1989

Sunflower Civic Center, Ramat Hasharon, 1990

Competition entry for New Acropolis Museum, Athens, 1990

ALL LOCATIONS ARE IN GERMANY

RON HERRON

Prospect County Secondary School, St. Pancras, London, 1958

Walking City, 1964

Instant City, 1968 (with Peter Cook and Dennis Crompton)

Competition entry for Casino, Monte Carlo, 1972
(first prize; with Archigram)

Library, Trondheim, Norway, 1977 (with Per Kartvedt)

Bubble Theater Company inflatable theater, London, 1978
(with Pentagram)

Competition entry for DOM Office Headquarters,
Cologne, Germany, 1981 (sixth prize; with Cook & Hawley)

Wonderworld Theme Park, Corby, Northamptonshire, England, 1981

Competition entry for La Défense, Paris, 1983 (with Warren Chalk)

Competition entry for The Peak, Hong Kong, 1983

Exhibition design, "Unity of Man," Commonwealth Institute, London,
1984 (with Richard Leakey)

Competition entry for L'Oreal Headquarters, Karlsruhe, Germany, 1988

Imagination Headquarters, Store Street, London, 1989

HOLT HINSHAW PFAU JONES

Competition entry for Pacific Center for the Media Arts,
Hawaii Loa College, Kaneohe, Oahu, 1987 (second prize)

Right Away Redy Mix 1 and 2 (cement factory),
Oakland, California, 1987

Altman & Manley Office, San Francisco, 1988

Overlake Sector Offices, Newark, California, 1988

Bridgeway Science and Industry Project, Newark, California, 1988

Competition entry for Warden's House, Alcatraz,
San Francisco Bay, California, 1989

Paramount Pictures Film and Tape Archives, Hollywood, California,
under construction 1990

Astronauts Memorial, Kennedy Space Center, Florida,
under construction 1990

Chiltern Estate, Northern California, under construction 1990

Chiller and Cogeneration Plant and Facilities Management Complex,
University of California, Los Angeles, 1991 (with Chas. T. Main, Inc.
engineers)

KAPLAN / KRUEGER

Project, "Homeless at Home" exhibition, Storefront for Art and
Architecture, New York, 1986

Project for ADPSR auction, Max Protetch Gallery,
New York, 1986

Project, "From Here to Eternity" exhibition, Artists Space Gallery,
New York, 1986

Installation, Art on the Beach, Long Island City, New York, 1987
(with J. Croak)

Unnamed Machine, "Installed Mechanisms" exhibition, Columbia
University, New York, 1987

"Spirit of Design," Interior Center, Tokyo, and University of Asahikawa,
Hokkaido, Japan, 1988

"Project DMZ" exhibition, Storefront for Art and Architecture,
New York, 1988

Renegade Cities, installation, Storefront for Art and Architecture,
New York, 1989

Avalanche City, installation, Artpark, Lewiston, New York, 1989

Bureau-Dicto City, 1989

CHRISTOPH LANGHOF

Gorlitzer Swimming Pools, Kreuzberg, Berlin, 1987

Competition entry for Berlin Skyscraper, 1988 (first prize)

Competition entry for Living on a Parking Garage, 1989

Copyworks Project, London, Paris, New York, Los Angeles, Tokyo,
and Berlin, 1989

L'Omnibus: A Forum for the Planet, "Paris: Architecture and Utopia"
exhibition, Pavillon de l'Arsenal, Paris, 1989

Horst Korber Sports Center, Berlin, 1990

DANIEL LIBESKIND

Three Machines for Palmanova: The Reading Machine, The Memory Machine (including the Cloud Machine), The Writing Machine, Venice Biennale, 1985

House without Walls, Milan Triennale, 1986

City Edge, housing and commercial project for the IBA, Flottwellstrasse, Berlin, 1987

Housing Villa, Lützowplatz, Berlin, 1988

New City Plan for Berlin, 1988

Yatai Architecture, Nagoya, Japan, 1988

Extension to Berlin Museum (including the Jewish Museum), 1989

Folly, Expo '90, Osaka, Japan, 1989

Urban Design for Potsdamer Platz, Berlin, 1989

CHRISTOPH MÄCKLER

Apartment House, Ruemerberg, 1980

Bureau de Change JSP KG, Düsseldorf, 1984

Renovation and extension of Computer Animation Laboratory, Frankfurt, 1986

Extension to German Federal Railway Administration Building, Berlin, 1986 (design study commissioned by the IBA)

House for the Representative of the Federal Republic of Germany, East Berlin, 1988

Family House, Kronberg, Taunus, 1989

Three train stations, Frankfurt, 1989

Bronner Publishing House Offices, Frankfurt, 1989 (project)

Central Offices, Frankfurt Airport, 1989 (project)

Multistory "Skyscraper," Eschersheimer Landstrasse/Adickesallee, Frankfurt, 1989

IMRE MAKOVECZ

Supermarket, Sárospatak, 1970

Cultural Center, Sárospatak, 1974/83

Birdwatch Tower, Tisza River, 1975 (project)

Mortuary Chapel, Farkasrét Cemetery, Budapest, 1977

Folk Art Center, Tokaj, 1980

Ski Station and Café, Dobogókö, 1980

Sports Center and Restaurant, Visegrád, 1980

Community Hall, Zalaszentlászló, 1983

Richter House, Budapest, 1985

Cultural Center, Jászkisér, 1985

Apartment Block, Sárospatak, 1987

Nature Education Center, Visegrád, 1988

Community House, Bak, 1988

Casino and Cultural Center, Szigetvár, 1988

Cultural Center, Bak, 1988

Roman Catholic Church, Paks, under construction 1990

MIRALLES AND PINÓS

Competition entry for Plaza Mayor, Alcaniz, 1983 (second prize)

Competition entry for Administrative Center, Lugo, 1984 (first prize)

Sunshade roofs, Plaza Mayor, Parets del Valles, Barcelona, 1985

Competition entry for Agricultural School, Realejos, Tenerife, 1985

Social Center, Hostalets, 1985 (project)

Competition entry for Congress of Deputies addition, Madrid, 1986

Competition entry for a development in Palma de Mallorca, 1986

Civic Center, Hostalets, 1986 (project)

Restoration of the Convent of the Trinity, Valencia, 1987

Competition entry for residential buildings, Joan Güell Street, Barcelona, 1987

La Lluana Boys School, Badelona, 1987

Confederation of Commerce, Barcelona, 1988

Javier Garau House, Barcelona, 1988

Project for Expo '92, Seville, 1988

Competition entry for Sports Palace, Huesca, 1988 (first prize)

Installations for the 1992 Olympic Games, Barcelona, 1989

Cemetery, Igualada, under construction 1990

M O R P H O S I S

2-4-6-8 House, Los Angeles, 1978

Sedlak Residence, Venice, California, 1980

Competition entry for Vietnam Veterans Memorial,
Washington, D.C., 1981

72 Market Street Restaurant, Venice, California, 1983

Hennessey and Ingalls Bookstore Facade,
Santa Monica, California, 1984

Kate Mantilini Restaurant, Los Angeles, 1986

Gonfiantini Residence (Reno House), Reno, Nevada, 1987 (project)

Contempo Casual Retail Store, Westwood, California, 1987

Crawford Residence, Montecito, California, 1988

Sixth Street House, Santa Monica, California, 1988

Vecta Showroom, West Hollywood, California, 1988

Competition entry for Berlin Wall, 1988

Chiba Golf Club, Tokyo, 1988

Competition entry for Berlin Library, 1988

Cedars-Sinai Comprehensive Cancer Center, Los Angeles, 1989

San Fernando Valley Arts Park, Performing Arts Center,
Los Angeles, under construction 1990

Humanities Building, Princeton University,
Princeton, New Jersey, under construction 1990

E R I C   O W E N   M O S S

Petal House, Los Angeles, 1984

Competition entry for New National Theater and Opera House,
Tokyo, 1986

Honey Springs Country Club, San Diego, California, 1987

Central Housing Office Building, University of California, Irvine, 1988

Lindblade Tower, Culver City, California, 1989

Paramount Laundry, Culver City, 1989

Samitaur Office Building, Culver City, under construction 1990

Weston/Lawson House, Los Angeles, under construction 1990

8522 National Boulevard, Culver City, under construction 1990

Gary Group Office Building, Culver City, under construction 1990

KIKOO MOZUNA

Anti-Dwelling Box (residence), Kushiro, Hokkaido, 1972

Uchu-an, Cosmic Hermitage I, II, III, 1975 (project)

Heaven-Man-Earth (three houses), Wakayama, Kyoto, and Koyasan, 1976

Ainu Folk Museum, Hokkaido, 1982

City Museum, Kushiro, Hokkaido, 1984

Marsh Museum, Kushiro, Hokkaido, 1984

Higashi Junior High School, Hokkaido, 1985

Competition entry for Information City, Kawasaki, 1987

Unoki Elementary School, Akita, 1988

Fisherman's Wharf, Hokkaido, 1990

CHRISTIAN DE PORTZAMPARC

Competition entry for Opera House, La Bastille, Paris, 1983

Erik Satie Conservatory and Residences for the Elderly, Paris, 1983

Residential Buildings, Lognes, Marne-la-Vallée, France, 1985

Beaubourg Café, Pompidou Center, Paris, 1986

Center for the Elderly, Paris, 1987

School of Dance, Paris Opera, Nanterre, France, 1987

Shop fittings for Emanuel Ungaro boutique, Paris, 1988

Hotel, EuroDisney, Marne-la-Vallée, 1988

City of Music, Parc de la Villette, Paris, under construction 1990

Residential Housing, Lützowstrasse, Berlin, under construction 1990

Urban Center, Nanterre, under construction 1990

ALL LOCATIONS ARE IN JAPAN

CEDRIC PRICE

Aviary, London Zoo, 1961 (with Lord Snowdon and Frank Newby)

Fun Palace, London, 1961 (project)

Potteries Thinkbelt, Staffordshire, England, 1964 (project)

Pop-up Parliament, 1965

Blackpool Zoological Gardens, Lancashire, England, 1971

Olympia Information Complex, Olympic Village, Munich, 1972

Trucksafe, Dock Ahoy, Air Portable, 1978 on (theoretical projects)

South Bank Development Plan for Greater London Council, 1983

Mark I Greenhouse, Parc de la Villette, Paris, 1987

Redevelopment of Congress Hall (with communications system), London, 1989

Duck Land Development, Hamburg, Germany, 1989

STANLEY SAITOWITZ

Brebnor House, Schoemansville, Transvaal, South Africa, 1976

Sundial House, Palomino Lakes, California, 1980

House at Florida Hills, Transvaal, 1981

Chabad House (synagogue addition), Berkeley, California, 1982

Quady Winery, Madera, California, 1983

Competition entry for Clos Pegase Winery, Napa, California, 1984

California Museum of Photography, Riverside, California, 1986

Grewal House, Oakland, California, 1987

McDonald House, Stinson Beach, California, 1987

Competition entry for the Berlin Library, 1988

Natoma Street Live/Work, San Francisco, 1989

Byron Meyer House, Napa, 1989

KAZUO SHINOHARA

House in Kugayama, Tokyo, 1954

Umbrella House, Tokyo, 1961

House with an Earthen Floor, Kita-saku, Nagano, 1963

House in White, Tokyo, 1966

House of Earth, Tokyo, 1966

Suzusho House, Miura, Kanagawa, 1968

Incomplete House, Tokyo, 1970

Shino House, Tokyo, 1970

Cubic Forest House, Kawasaki, Kanagawa, 1971

Tanikawa Residence, Naganohara, Gunma, 1975

House in Uehara, Tokyo, 1976

House Under High-Voltage Lines, Tokyo, 1981

Ukiyo-e Museum, Matsumoto, 1982

House in Yokohama, 1984

Centennial Anniversary Hall, Tokyo Institute of Technology, 1988

SZYSZKOWITZ + KOWALSKI

House Above Graz, Austria, 1975

Grunes House, Graz, 1979

Conversion of Schloss Grosslobming into a business college, Grosslobming, Austria, 1981

Forestry School, Schloss Pichl, Mitterdorf/Murztal, Austria, 1984

Apartment House, Alte Poststrasse, Graz, 1984

Rotes House, Graz, 1984

Housing, Eisbach-Rein, Austria, 1986

Church Complex, Graz-Ragnitz, Austria, 1986

Houses at Knittelfeld, Austria, 1987

House in Harmisch, Austria, 1988

House V, Wien-Hietzing, Austria, 1988

Competition entry for German Rheumatism Research Center, Berlin, 1988 (first prize)

Experimental housing project for International Garden Exhibition '93, Stuttgart, Germany, 1989

TEAM ZOO

Master Plan, Nago, Japan, 1973

Master Plan, Nakijin, Japan, 1974

Domo Arabeska (residence), Tokyo, 1974

Domo Serakanto (residence), Kamakura, Japan, 1974

Central Community Hall, Nakijin, 1975

City Hall, Nago, 1978

Shirahama Park, Ishikawa, Japan, 1978

Shinshukan Community Center, Miyashiro, Japan, 1980

Kasahara Elementary School, Miyashiro, 1982

Agricultural Cooperative Community Center, Asa, Japan, 1985

House at Natsumidai, Japan, 1985

Yoga Promenade, Tokyo, 1986

Rapporo Russian Hall, Urahoro, Hokkaido, Japan,
under construction 1990

Ilan County Hall, Lotung, Taiwan, under construction 1990

D. + R. THUT

Apartment House, Genterstrasse, Munich, 1969–71

Entry for "Integra" competition, prefabricated urban construction, 1972

Apartment House, Munich-Perlach, Germany, 1975–78

Pasing Squash Sports Hall, Munich, 1979–80

Apartment House, Benglen, Switzerland, 1979–81

Vini and Olii Wine Cellar, Munich, 1983

Public Housing, Max Planck Strasse, Erding, Germany, 1982–84

Competition entry for Parkhaus Hammerweg,
Rosenheim, Germany, 1986

Competition entry for Information City, Kawasaki, Japan, 1987

Competition entry for Public Housing, Salzburg, Austria,
1987 (first prize)

Steinberger Residence, Hafbauernstrasse, Munich, 1986–88

BERNARD TSCHUMI

Parc de la Villette, Paris, 1983–90

Competition entry for New National Theater and Opera House, Tokyo, 1986 (second prize)

Strasbourg County Hall, France, 1986

Conceptual plan for Flushing Meadows–Corona Park, New York, 1987–89

Hotel, EuroDisney, Marne-la-Vallée, France, 1988 (project)

Rotterdam Railway Tunnel Site, urban design proposal for Rotterdam, Netherlands, 1988

Moabiter Werder, urban and landscape design proposal, Berlin, 1988

Competition entry for Berlin Library, 1988

Ponts-Villes, Lausanne, Switzerland, 1988

Competition entry for New Kansai International Airport, Osaka, Japan, 1988 (second prize)

Vieux-Port, Montreal, 1989 (planning study)

Competition entry for National Library of France, Paris, 1989

Competition entry for ZKM Center for Art and Media Technology, Karlsruhe, Germany, 1989 (third prize)

Steelworks, Völklingen, Germany, 1989 (planning study)

ARBED Headquarters, Esch, Luxembourg, 1990

MICHAEL WEBB

Furniture Manufacturers' Association Headquarters, 1957

Sin Palace, 1962–64

Drive-in Housing, 1964–66

Cushicle/Suitaloon, 1967–69

Brünhilde's Magic Ring of Fire, 1970

Dreams Come True, 1971

Forest Murmurs/Maida Vale Bombed, 1974

Temple Island, 1976–84

PETER WILSON

Pont des Arts, Paris, 1982

Competition entry for Accademia Bridge, Venice Biennale, 1985

Paradiso Bridge, Amsterdam, 1986 (project)

Competition entry for New National Theater and Opera House, Tokyo, 1986

Blackburn House, London, 1986

Rotterdam Railway Tunnel Site, urban design proposal for Rotterdam, Netherlands, 1988

Rosslyn Mews, London, 1988 (with Chassay Wright)

Forum of Sand, Berlin, 1988 (project)

Kindergarten, Frankfurt, Germany, 1988

Competition entry for "Comfort in the Metropolis," 1988.

Folly, Expo '90, Osaka, Japan, 1989

Competition entry for ZKM Center for Art and Media Technology, Karlsruhe, Germany, 1989 (second prize)

Green Homes Offices, Cosmos Street, Tokyo, 1989

Bridge Fort, Asperen, Netherlands, 1989

Competition entry for Kassel Sculpture Hall, Germany, 1989

City Library, Münster, Germany, under construction 1990

WOOD / MARSH

Extension to Frantzeskos House, Eaglemont, Australia, 1983

S.M.R. Audio-Visual Recording Studios, St. Kilda, Australia, 1983

Inflation Nightclub, Melbourne, Australia, 1984

Sub-Terrain Nightclub, Melbourne, 1984

Choong House, Eltham, Australia, 1985

Cherrylane Headquarters, New York, 1986

Macrae & Way Film Production Studio, South Melbourne, 1986

Luxaflex Showroom and Offices, West Melbourne, 1987

Babic House, Mount Martha, Australia, 1988

Installation for Stieg Persson exhibition, City Gallery, Melbourne, 1988

Set design, "Design for Australian Living" exhibition, Australian Center for Contemporary Art, Melbourne, 1988

Toscani's Café/Bar/Restaurant, Melbourne, 1988

Nine-Story Office Building, Russell Street, Melbourne, 1988 (project)

Tweedie Gallery, Richmond, Australia, 1989

LEBBEUS WOODS

Einstein Tomb, 1980

Four Cities, 1981

Center for New Technology, 1983

Epicyclarium, 1984

A. City, 1986

Aeroliving-laboratories, 1987

Centricity Freespace, 1988

Underground Berlin, 1988

Terra Nova, 1988

Solohouse, 1989

Aerial Paris Project, 1989

KLAUS ZILLICH

Competition entry for Prince Albrecht Palace, Berlin, 1984
(with Rebecca Horn and Jasper Halfmann)

Cosmological Park (Calendar Square, Café Orangerie, and Rhizomatic
Bridge), Berlin, 1984–85 (with Halfmann and Zilling)

Competition entry for Film Center Esplanade, Berlin, 1985
(first prize; with Halfmann)

Competition entry for Platz der Republik, Berlin, 1986
(with Halfmann and FPB)

Grand Gallery of Painting, Berlin, 1987

Competition entry for Landugsbrucken, Hamburg, Germany, 1987
(third prize)

Central Library, Technical University and École Supérieure des Beaux-
Arts, Berlin, 1988 (project; with Engel)

LTTC Rot-Weiss Tennis Club and Press Center, Berlin, 1988–91

Competition entry for Ortolanweg Cooperative Housing, Berlin, 1989
(special prize; with Engel)

Apartment House, Block 19, Berlin, under construction 1990

Nursery School, Lützowstrasse, Berlin, under construction 1990

Nursery School, Lindauer Allee, Berlin, under construction 1990

PHOTOGRAPHY CREDITS

All photographs are provided courtesy of the architects. Individual photographers are credited below.

HA
INTROD

STÉPHANE
CHRISTIAN DE PORTZAMPA

NICOLAS BOREL
CHRISTIAN DE PORTZAMPARC |5 |6 |7 |8

ZEL COOK/AA LONDON
UCTION |3

COUTUR
ARC |2 |3

W. GRÖSCHEL / MUNICH
D. + R. THUT ____1| ___2| ___4| |5

GARY LEWIS GURRIA
MICHAEL WEBB ____1| |2 |3 |4 |5

TERRY HOPE
RON HERRON |1 |6 |8

WILMAR KOENIG / BERLIN
CHRISTOPH LANGHOF ____1| 2| |3 |4 |5
KLAUS ZILLICH |6

JEAN BIAUGEAUD
ALSOP AND LYALL |3

WALTRAUD KRASE / FRANKFURT
CHRISTOPH MÄCKLER |1   2| 3| |6

TOM BONNER / LOS ANGELES
COOP HIMMELBLAU   5| 6| |7
MORPHOSIS   2| |3 |4 |5 |6 |7
ERIC OWEN MOSS ___7| 8| |9 |10

HEINER LEISKA
EISELE + FRITZ   5|

J. LITTKEMAN / BERLIN

CHRISTOPH LANGHOF ___6|

MARK LIVERMORE

RON HERRON ___3| |5 ___7|

MITSUO MATSUOKA / SHINKENCHIKU

KIKOO MOZUNA |7___

PETER MAUSS / ESTO

FRANK GEHRY ___5| ___6| |8

GRANT MUDFORD

MORPHOSIS |8___

SIGRID NEUBERT

D. + R. THUT ___3|

K. PARIKH / AA LONDON

INTRODUCTION |11

UWE RAU / BERLIN

KLAUS ZILLICH |5___

PAOLO ROSSELLI / MILAN

SANTIAGO CALATRAVA ___1| ‾2| ___3| |4 ___5| ‾6|

SEIHAN SATOH

KIKOO MOZUNA |1‾ |2___ ___3| |4 ‾5| |6 |8 ___9|

TIM STREET-PORTER

ERIC OWEN MOSS ___1|

A. C. THEIL

JASPER HALFMANN ___2|

E. VALENTINE-HAMES

BRANSON COATES |4‾ |5‾

ALEX VERTIKOFF

ERIC OWEN MOSS ___2| ‾3| |4

DEIDI VON SCHAWEN

CHRISTIAN DE PORTZAMPARC ___1|

DOUGLAS WHYTE

ASYMPTOTE |1‾ ___4|

GERALD ZUGMANN / VIENNA

COOP HIMMELBLAU |1‾ |2___ |3‾